Lucio to the spot where he had left Mellida, learns from Andrugio's page that she has been carried away. Andrugio now separates himself from Antonio and Lucio; proceeds, clad in a complete suit of armour, to the court of Piero, and announces that he has come to claim the reward offered for Andrugio's head. Piero declares his willingness to pay the reward; and then Andrugio, raising his beaver, discovers himself to Piero and the assembled courtiers. Piero affects to be struck with admiration for his adversary's magnanimity, and professes friendship for the future. A funeral procession now enters, followed by Lucio, who announces that he has brought the body of Antonio. Andrugio mourns for the death of his son and Piero affects to share his grief, protesting that he would give his own life or his daughter's hand to purchase breath for the dead man. Thereupon Antonio, who had died only in conceit, rises from the bier and claims the hand of Mellida. Piero assents, and the First Part of Antonio and Mellida closes joyfully.

To the only rewarder and most just poiser of virtuous merits, the most honourably renowned Nobody, bounteous Mecænas of poetry and Lord Protector of oppressed innocence, do dedicoque.

Since it hath flowed with the current of my humorous blood to affect (a little too much) to be seriously fantastical, here take (most respected Patron) the worthless present of my slighter idleness. If you vouchsafe not his protection, then, O thou sweetest perfection (Female Beauty), shield me from the stopping of vinegar bottles. Which most wished favour if it fail me, then Si nequeo flectere superos, Acheronta movebo. But yet, honour's redeemer, virtue's advancer, religion's shelter, and piety's fosterer, yet, yet, I faint not in despair of thy gracious affection and protection; to which I only shall ever rest most servingman-like, obsequiously making legs and standing (after our free-born English garb) bareheaded. Thy only affied slave and admirer,

J. M.

I0163623

DRAMATIS PERSONÆ
Piero Sforza, Duke of Venice.
Andrugio, Duke of Genoa.
Antonio, son to Andrugio, in love with Mellida.
Feliche, a high-minded courtier.
Alberto, a Venetian gentleman, in love with Rossaline.
Balurdo, a rich gull.
Matzagente, a modern braggadoch, son to the Duke of Milan.
Galeatzo, son to the Duke of Florence, a suitor to Mellida.
Forobosco, a Parasite.
Castilio Balthazar, a spruce courtier.
Lucio, an old nobleman, friend to Andrugio.
Catzo, page to Castilio.
Dildo, page to Balurdo.
Painter, Andrugio's page, &c.
Mellida, daughter to Piero, in love with Antonio.
Rossaline, niece to Piero.
Flavia, a waiting-woman.

SCENE:—Venice and the Neighbourhood.

INDUCTION

Enter **GALEATZO, PIERO, ALBERTO, ANTONIO, FOROBOSCO, BALURDO, MATZAGENTE**, and **FELICHE**, with parts in their hands; having cloaks cast over their apparel.

GALEATZO
Come, sirs, come! the music will sound straight for entrance. Are ye ready, are ye perfect?

PIERO
Faith! we can say our parts; but we are ignorant in what mould we must cast our actors.

ALBERTO
Whom do you personate?

PIERO
Piero, Duke of Venice.

ALBERTO
O! ho! then thus frame your exterior shape
To haughty form of elate majesty,
As if you held the palsy-shaking head
Of reeling chance under your fortune's belt
In strictest vassalage: grow big in thought,
As swoln with glory of successful arms.

PIERO
If that be all, fear not; I'll suit it right.
Who cannot be proud, stroke up the hair, and strut?

ALBERTO
Truth; such rank custom is grown popular;
And now the vulgar fashion strides as wide,
And stalks as proud upon the weakest stilts
Of the slight'st fortunes, as if Hercules
Or burly Atlas shoulder'd up their state.

PIERO
Good: but whom act you?

ALBERTO
The necessity of the play forceth me to act two parts: Andrugio, the distressed Duke of Genoa, and Alberto, a Venetian gentleman, enamoured on the Lady Rossaline; whose fortunes being too weak to sustain the port of her, he proved always disastrous in love; his worth being much underpoised by the uneven scale, that currents all things by the outward stamp of opinion.

GALEATZO
Well, and what dost thou play?

BALURDO
The part of all the world.

ALBERTO
The part of all the world? What's that?

BALURDO
The fool. Ay, in good deed law now, I play Balurdo, a wealthy mountbanking burgomasco's heir of Venice.

ALBERTO
Ha! ha! one whose foppish nature might seem great, only for wise men's recreation; and, like a juiceless bark, to preserve the sap of more strenuous spirits. A servile hound, that loves the scent of forerunning fashion, like an empty hollow vault, still giving an echo to wit: greedily champing what any other well valued judgment had beforehand chew'd.

FOROBOSCO
Ha! ha! ha! tolerably good, good faith, sweet wag.

ALBERTO
Umph; why tolerably good, good faith, sweet wag? Go, go; you flatter me.

FOROBOSCO
Right; I but dispose my speech to the habit of my part.

ALBERTO
Why, what plays he?

[To **FELICHE**.

FELICHE
The wolf that eats into the breasts of princes; that breeds the lethargy and falling sickness in honour; makes justice look asquint; and blinds the eye of merited reward from viewing desertful virtue.

ALBERTO
What's all this periphrasis, ha?

FELICHE
The substance of a supple-chapt flatterer.

ALBERTO
O! doth he play Forobosco the Parasite? Good, i'faith. Sirrah, you must seem now as glib and straight in outward semblance as a lady's busk, though inwardly as cross as a pair of tailors' legs; having a tongue

as nimble as his needle, with servile patches of glavering flattery to stitch up the bracks of unworthily honour'd—

FOROBOSCO
I warrant you, I warrant you, you shall see me prove the very periwig to cover the bald pate of brainless gentility. Ho! I will so tickle the sense of bella gratiosa madonna with the titillation of hyperbolical praise, that I'll strike it in the nick, in the very nick, chuck.

FELICHE [To **ANTONIO**]
Thou promisest more than I hope any spectator gives faith of performance; but why look you so dusky, ha?

ANTONIO
I was never worse fitted since the nativity of my actorship; I shall be hiss'd at, on my life now.

FELICHE
Why, what must you play?

ANTONIO
Faith, I know not what; an hermaphrodite, two parts in one; my true person being Antonio, son to the Duke of Genoa; though for the love of Mellida, Piero's daughter, I take this feigned presence of an Amazon, calling myself Florizell, and I know not what. I a voice to play a lady! I shall ne'er do it.

ALBERTO
O! an Amazon should have such a voice, virago-like. Not play two parts in one? away, away, 'tis common fashion. Nay, if you cannot bear two subtle fronts under one hood, idiot, go by, go by, off this world's stage! O time's impurity!

ANTONIO
Ay, but when use hath taught me action
To hit the right point of a lady's part,
I shall grow ignorant, when I must turn
Young prince again, how but to truss my hose.

FELICHE
Tush, never put them off; for women wear the breeches still.

MATZAGENTE
By the bright honour of a Milanoise,
And the resplendent fulgor of this steel,
I will defend the feminine to death,
And ding his spirit to the verge of hell,
That dares divulge a lady's prejudice!

[Exeunt **MATZAGENTE**, **FOROBOSCO**, and **BALURDO**.

FELICHE
Rampum scrampum, mount tufty Tamburlaine!

What rattling thunderclap breaks from his lips?

ALBERTO
O! 'tis native to his part. For acting a modern braggadoch under the person of Matzagente, the Duke of Milan's son, it may seem to suit with good fashion of coherence.

PIERO
But methinks he speaks with a spruce Attic accent of adulterate Spanish.

ALBERTO
So 'tis resolv'd. For Milan being half Spanish, half high Dutch, and half Italians, the blood of chiefest houses is corrupt and mongrel'd; so that you shall see a fellow vain-glorious for a Spaniard, gluttonous for a Dutchman, proud for an Italian, and a fantastic idiot for all. Such a one conceit this Matzagente.

FELICHE
But I have a part allotted me, which I have neither able apprehension to conceit, nor what I conceit gracious ability to utter.

GALEATZO
Whoop, in the old cut! Good, show us a draught of thy spirit.

FELICHE
'Tis steady and must seem so impregnably fortressed with his own content that no envious thought could ever invade his spirit; never surveying any man so unmeasuredly happy, whom I thought not justly hateful for some true impoverishment; never beholding any favour of Madam Felicity gracing another, which his well-bounded content persuaded not to hang in the front of his own fortune; and therefore as far from envying any man, as he valued all men infinitely distant from accomplished beatitude. These native adjuncts appropriate to me the name of Feliche. But last, good, thy humour.

[Exeunt **PIERO**, **ALBERTO**, and **GALEATZO**.

ANTONIO
'Tis to be described by signs and tokens. For unless I were possessed with a legion of spirits, 'tis impossible to be made perspicuous by any utterance: for sometimes he must take austere state, as for the person of Galeatzo, the son of the Duke of Florence, and possess his exterior presence with a formal majesty: keep popularity in distance, and on the sudden fling his honour so prodigally into a common arm, that he may seem to give up his indiscretion to the mercy of vulgar censure. Now as solemn as a traveller, and as grave as a Puritan's ruff; with the same breath as slight and scattered in his fashion as a—a—anything; now as sweet and neat as a barber's casting-bottle; straight as slovenly as the yeasty breast of an ale-knight: now lamenting, then chafing, straight laughing, then—

FELICHE
What then?

ANTONIO
Faith, I know not what; 't had been a right part for Proteus or Gew. Ho! blind Gew would ha' done 't rarely, rarely.

FELICHE

I fear it is not possible to limn so many persons in so small a tablet as the compass of our plays afford.

ANTONIO

Right! therefore I have heard that those persons, as he and you, Feliche, that are but slightly drawn in this comedy, should receive more exact accomplishment in a second part; which, if this obtain gracious acceptance, means to try his fortune.

FELICHE

Peace, here comes the Prologue: clear the stage.

[Exeunt.

THE PROLOGUE

The wreath of pleasure and delicious sweets,
Begirt the gentle front of this fair troop!
Select and most respected auditors,
For wit's sake do not dream of miracles.
Alas! we shall but falter, if you lay
The least sad weight of an unusèd hope
Upon our weakness; only we give up
The worthless present of slight idleness
To your authentic censure. O! that our Muse
Had those abstruse and sinewy faculties,
That, with a strain of fresh invention,
She might press out the rarity of Art;
The pur'st elixèd juice of rich conceit
In your attentive ears; that with the lip
Of gracious elocution we might drink
A sound carouse into your health of wit.
But O! the heavy dryness of her brain,
Foil to your fertile spirits, is asham'd
To breathe her blushing numbers to such ears.
Yet (most ingenious) deign to veil our wants;
With sleek acceptance polish these rude scenes;
And if our slightness your large hope beguiles,
Check not with bended brow, but dimpled smiles.

[Exit **PROLOGUE**.

THE FIRST PART OF ANTONIO AND MELLIDA

ACT I

SCENE I

Neighbourhood of Venice.

The cornets sound a battle within.

Enter **ANTONIO**, disguised like an Amazon.

ANTONIO
Heart, wilt not break? and thou abhorrèd life,
Wilt thou still breathe in my enragèd blood?
Veins, sinews, arteries, why crack ye not,
Burst and divulst with anguish of my grief?
Can man by no means creep out of himself,
And leave the slough of viperous grief behind?
Antonio, hast thou seen a fight at sea,
As horrid as the hideous day of doom,
Betwixt thy father, Duke of Genoa,
And proud Piero, the Venetian Prince:
In which the sea hath swoln with Genoa's blood,
And made spring-tides with the warm reeking gore,
That gush'd from out our galleys' scupper-holes?
In which thy father, poor Andrugio,
Lies sunk, or leap'd into the arms of chance,
Choked with the labouring ocean's brackish foam;
Who, even despite Piero's canker'd hate,
Would with an armèd hand have seized thy love,
And link'd thee to the beauteous Mellida.
Have I outlived the death of all these hopes?
Have I felt anguish pour'd into my heart,
Burning like balsamum in tender wounds!
And yet dost live! Could not the fretting sea
Have roll'd me up in wrinkles of his brow?
Is death grown coy, or grim confusion nice,
That it will not accompany a wretch,
But I must needs be cast on Venice' shore,
And try new fortunes with this strange disguise
To purchase my adorèd Mellida?

[The cornets sound a flourish; cease.

Hark how Piero's triumphs beat the air!
O, rugged mischief, how thou grat'st my heart!—
Take spirit, blood; disguise, be confident;
Make a firm stand; here rests the hope of all:
Lower than hell, there is no depth to fall.

[The cornets sound a senet. Enter **FELICHE** and **ALBERTO**, **CASTILIO** and **FOROBOSCO**, a **PAGE** carrying a shield; **PIERO** in armour; **CATZO** and **DILDO** and **BALURDO**. All these, saving **PIERO**, armed with petronels. Being entered, they make a stand in divided files.

PIERO
Victorious Fortune, with triumphant hand,
Hurleth my glory 'bout this ball of earth,
Whilst the Venetian Duke is heavèd up
On wings of fair success, to overlook
The low-cast ruins of his enemies,
To see myself adored and Genoa quake;
My fate is firmer than mischance can shake.

FELICHE
Stand; the ground trembleth.

PIERO
Ha! an earthquake?

BALURDO
O! I smell a sound.

FELICHE
Piero, stay, for I descry a fume
Creeping from out the bosom of the deep,
The breath of darkness, fatal when 'tis wist
In greatness' stomach. This same smoke, call'd pride,
Take heed: she'll lift thee to improvidence,
And break thy neck from steep security;
She'll make thee grudge to let Jehovah share
In thy successful battles. O! she's ominous;
Enticeth princes to devour heaven,
Swallow omnipotence, out-stare dread fate,
Subdue eternity in giant thought;
Heaves up their heart with swelling, puff'd conceit,
Till their souls burst with venom'd arrogance.
Beware, Piero; Rome itself hath tried,
Confusion's train blows up this Babel pride.

PIERO
Pish! Dimitto superos, summa votorum attigi.
Alberto, hast thou yielded up our fix'd decree
Unto the Genoan ambassador?
Are they content, if that their Duke return,
To send his and his son Antonio's head,
As pledges steep'd in blood, to gain their peace?

ALBERTO

With most obsequious sleek-brow'd entertain,
They all embrace it as most gracious.

PIERO
Are proclamations sent through Italy,
That whosoever brings Andrugio's head,
Or young Antonio's, shall be guerdonèd
With twenty thousand double pistolets,
And be endearèd to Piero's love?

FOROBOSCO
They are sent every way: sound policy,
Sweet lord.

FELICHE [Aside]
Confusion to these limber sycophants!
No sooner mischiefs born in regency,
But flattery christens it with policy.

PIERO
Why, then,—O me cœlitum excelsissimum!
The intestine malice and inveterate hate
I always bore to that Andrugio,
Glories in triumph o'er his misery;
Nor shall that carpet-boy Antonio
Match with my daughter, sweet-cheek'd Mellida.
No; the public power makes my faction strong.

FELICHE
Ill, when public power strength'neth private wrong.

PIERO
'Tis horse-like not for man to know his force.

FELICHE
'Tis god-like for a man to feel remorse.

PIERO
Pish! I prosecute my family's revenge,
Which I'll pursue with such a burning chase,
Till I have dried up all Andrugio's blood;
Weak rage, that with slight pity is withstood.—

[The cornets sound a flourish.

What means that fresh triumphal flourish sound?

ALBERTO

The prince of Milan, and young Florence' heir,
Approach to gratulate your victory.

PIERO
We'll girt them with an ample waste of love.
Conduct them to our presence royally;
Let vollies of the great artillery
From off our galleys' banks play prodigal,
And sound loud welcome from their bellowing mouths.

[Exeunt all but **PIERO**.

[The cornets sound a senet. Enter above, **MELLIDA**, **ROSSALINE**, and **FLAVIA**. Enter below, **GALEATZO**
with **ATTENDANTS**; **PIERO** meeteth him, embraceth; at which the cornets sound a flourish; **PIERO** and
GALEATZO exeunt; the rest stand still.

MELLIDA
What prince was that passed through my father's guard?

FLAVIA
'Twas Galeatzo, the young Florentine.

ROSSALINE
Troth, one that will besiege thy maidenhead;
Enter the walls, i'faith (sweet Mellida),
If that thy flankers be not cannon-proof.

MELLIDA
O, Mary Ambree, good, thy judgment, wench?
Thy bright election's clear: what will he prove?

ROSSALINE
Hath a short finger and a naked chin,
A skipping eye; dare lay my judgment (faith)
His love is glibbery; there's no hold on't, wench.
Give me a husband whose aspect is firm;
A full-cheek'd gallant with a bouncing thigh:
O, he is the Paradizo dell madonne contento.

MELLIDA
Even such a one was my Antonio.

[The cornets sound a senet.

ROSSALINE
By my nine and thirtieth servant, sweet,
Thou art in love; but stand on tiptoe, fair;
Here comes Saint Tristram Tirlery Whiffe, i'faith.

[Enter **MATZAGENTE**; **PIERO** meets him, embraceth; at which the cornets sound a flourish: they two stand, using seeming compliments, whilst the scene passeth above.

MELLIDA
St. Mark, St. Mark! what kind of thing appears?

ROSSALINE
For fancy's passion, spit upon him! Fie,
His face is varnish'd. In the name of love,
What country bred that creature?

MELLIDA
What is he, Flavia?

FLAVIA
The heir of Milan, Signior Matzagente.

ROSSALINE
Matzagente! now, by my pleasure's hope,
He is made like a tilting-staff; and looks
For all the world like an o'er-roasted pig:
A great tobacco-taker too, that's flat;
For his eyes look as if they had been hung
In the smoke of his nose.

MELLIDA
What husband will he prove, sweet Rossaline?

ROSSALINE
Avoid him; for he hath a dwindled leg,
A low forehead, and a thin coal-black beard;
And will be jealous too, believe it, sweet;
For his chin sweats, and hath a gander neck,
A thin lip, and a little monkish eye.
'Precious! what a slender waist he hath!
He looks like a may-pole, or a notched stick;
He'll snap in two at every little strain.
Give me a husband that will fill mine arms,
Of steady judgment, quick and nimble sense;
Fools relish not a lady's excellence.

[Exeunt **ALL** on the lower stage; at which the cornets sound a flourish, and a peal of shot is given.

MELLIDA
The triumph's ended; but look, Rossaline!
What gloomy soul in strange accustrements
Walks on the pavement?

ROSSALINE
Good sweet, let's to her; prithee, Mellida.

MELLIDA
How covetous thou art of novelties!

ROSSALINE
Pish! 'tis our nature to desire things
That are thought strangers to the common cut.

MELLIDA
I am exceeding willing, but—

ROSSALINE
But what? prithee, go down; let's see her face:
God send that neither wit nor beauty wants,
Those tempting sweets, affection's adamants.

[Exeunt.

ANTONIO
Come down: she comes like—O, no simile
Is precious, choice, or elegant enough
To illustrate her descent! Leap heart, she comes!
She comes! smile heaven, and softest southern wind
Kiss her cheek gently with perfumèd breath.
She comes! creation's purity, admir'd,
Ador'd amazing rarity, she comes!
O, now, Antonio, press thy spirit forth
In following passion, knit thy senses close,
Heap up thy powers, double all thy man.

[Enter **MELLIDA**, **ROSSALINE**, and **FLAVIA**.

She comes!
O, how her eyes dart wonder on my heart!
Mount blood! soul to my lips! taste Hebe's cup:
Stand firm on deck, when beauty's close fight's up.

MELLIDA
Lady, your strange habit doth beget
Our pregnant thoughts, even great of much desire,
To be acquaint with your condition.

ROSSALINE
Good, sweet lady, without more ceremonies,
What country claims your birth? and, sweet, your name?

ANTONIO

In hope your bounty will extend itself
In self-same nature of fair courtesy,
I'll shun all niceness; my name's Florizell,
My country Scythia; I am Amazon,
Cast on this shore by fury of the sea.

ROSSALINE

Nay, faith, sweet creature, we'll not veil our names.
It pleas'd the font to dip me Rossaline;
That lady bears the name of Mellida,
The Duke of Venice' daughter.

ANTONIO

Madam, I am oblig'd to kiss your hand,
By imposition of a now dead man.

[To **MELLIDA**, kissing her hand.

ROSSALINE

Now, by my troth, I long, beyond all thought,
To know the man; sweet beauty, deign his name.

ANTONIO

Lady, the circumstance is tedious.

ROSSALINE

Troth, not a whit; good fair, let's have it all:
I love not, I, to have a jot left out,
If the tale come from a loved orator.

ANTONIO

Vouchsafe me, then, your hush'd observances.—
Vehement in pursuit of strange novelties,
After long travel through the Asian main,
I shipp'd my hopeful thoughts for Brittany;
Longing to view great Nature's miracle,
The glory of our sex, whose fame doth strike
Remotest ears with adoration.
Sailing some two months with inconstant winds,
We view'd the glistering Venetian forts,
To which we made: when lo! some three leagues off,
We might descry a horrid spectacle;
The issue of black fury strew'd the sea
With tatter'd carcasses of splitted ships,
Half sinking, burning, floating topsy-turvy.
Not far from these sad ruins of fell rage,

We might behold a creature press the waves;
Senseless he sprawl'd, all notch'd with gaping wounds.
To him we made, and (short) we took him up;
The first thing he spake was,—Mellida!
And then he swooned.

MELLIDA
Ay me!

ANTONIO
Why sigh you, fair?

MELLIDA
Nothing but little humours; good sweet, on.

ANTONIO
His wounds being dress'd, and life recoverèd,
We 'gan discourse; when lo! the sea grew mad,
His bowels rumbling with wind-passion;
Straight swarthy darkness popp'd out Phœbus' eye,
And blurr'd the jocund face of bright-cheek'd day;
Whilst crudled fogs masked even darkness' brow:
Heaven bad's good night, and the rocks groan'd
At the intestine uproar of the main.
Now gusty flaws strook up the very heels
Of our mainmast, whilst the keen lightning shot
Through the black bowels of the quaking air;
Straight chops a wave, and in his sliftred paunch
Down falls our ship, and there he breaks his neck;
Which in an instant up was belkt again.
When thus this martyr'd soul began to sigh:
"Give me your hand (quoth he): now do you grasp
Th' unequall'd mirror of ragg'd misery:
Is't not a horrid storm? O, well-shaped sweet,
Could your quick eye strike through these gashèd wounds,
You should behold a heart, a heart, fair creature,
Raging more wild than is this frantic sea.
Wolt do me a favour? if thou chance survive,
But visit Venice, kiss the precious white
Of my most,—nay, all epithets are base
To attribute to gracious Mellida:
Tell her the spirit of Antonio
Wisheth his last gasp breath'd upon her breast."

ROSSALINE
Why weeps soft-hearted Florizell?

ANTONIO

Alas, the flinty rocks groan'd at his plaints.
"Tell her, (quoth he) that her obdurate sire
Hath crack'd his bosom;" therewithal he wept,
And thus sigh'd on: "The sea is merciful;
Look how it gapes to bury all my grief!
Well, thou shalt have it, thou shalt be his tomb:
My faith in my love live; in thee, die woe;
Die, unmatch'd anguish, die, Antonio!"
With that he totter'd from the reeling deck,
And down he sunk.

ROSSALINE
Pleasure's body! what makes my Lady weep?

MELLIDA
Nothing, sweet Rossaline, but the air's sharp —
My father's palace, Madam, will be proud
To entertain your presence, if you'll deign
To make repose within. Ay me!

ANTONIO
Lady, our fashion is not curious.

ROSSALINE
'Faith, all the nobler, 'tis more generous.

MELLIDA
Shall I then know how fortune fell at last,
What succour came, or what strange fate ensued?

ANTONIO
Most willingly: but this same court is vast,
And public to the staring multitude.

ROSSALINE
Sweet Lady, nay good sweet, now by my troth
We'll be bedfellows: dirt on compliment froth!

[Exeunt; **ROSSALINE** giving **ANTONIO** the way.

ACT II

SCENE I

Palace of the Duke of Venice.

Enter **CATZO**, with a capon eating; **DILDO** following him.

DILDO
Hah, Catzo, your master wants a clean trencher: do you hear?
Balurdo calls for your diminutive attendance.

CATZO
The belly hath no ears, Dildo.

DILDO
Good pug, give me some capon.

CATZO
No capon, no not a bit, ye smooth bully; capon's no meat for Dildo: milk, milk, ye glibbery urchin, is food
for infants.

DILDO
Upon mine honour.

CATZO
Your honour with a paugh! 'slid, now every jackanapes loads his back with the golden coat of honour;
every ass puts on the lion's skin and roars his honour. Upon your honour? By my lady's pantable, I fear I
shall live to hear a vintner's boy cry, "'Tis rich neat canary." Upon my honour!

DILDO
My stomach's up.

CATZO
I think thou art hungry.

DILDO
The match of fury is lighted, fastened to the linstock of rage, and will presently set fire to the touch-hole
of intemperance, discharging the double culverin of my incensement in the face of thy opprobrious
speech.

CATZO
I'll stop the barrel thus: good Dildo, set not fire to the touch-hole.

DILDO
My rage is stopp'd, and I will eat to the health of the fool, thy master Castilio.

CATZO
And I will suck the juice of the capon, to the health of the idiot, thy master Balurdo.

DILDO
Faith, our masters are like a case of rapiers sheathed in one scabbard of folly.

CATZO

Right Dutch blades. But was't not rare sport at the sea-battle, whilst rounce robble hobble roared from the ship-sides, to view our masters pluck their plumes and drop their feathers, for fear of being men of mark.

DILDO
'Slud (cried Signior Balurdo), O for Don Rosicleer's armour, in the Mirror of Knighthood! what coil's here? O for an armour, cannon-proof! O, more cable, more featherbeds! more featherbeds, more cable! till he had as much as my cable-hatband to fence him.

[Enter **FLAVIA** in haste, with a rebato.

CATZO
Buxom Flavia, can you sing? song, song!

FLAVIA
My sweet Dildo, I am not for you at this time: Madam Rossaline stays for a fresh ruff to appear in the presence: sweet, away.

DILDO
'Twill not be so put off, delicate, delicious, spark-eyed, sleek-skinn'd, slender-waisted, clean-legg'd, rarely-shaped—

FLAVIA
Who? I'll be at all your service another season: my faith, there's reason in all things.

DILDO
Would I were reason then, that I might be in all things.

CATZO
The breve and the semiquaver is, we must have the descant you made upon our names, ere you depart.

FLAVIA
Faith, the song will seem to come off hardly.

CATZO
Troth not a wit, if you seem to come off quickly.

FLAVIA
Pert Catzo, knock it lustily then.

[A song.

[Enter **FOROBOSCO**, with two torches: **CASTILIO** singing fantastically; **ROSSALINE** running a coranto pace, and **BALURDO**; **FELICHE** following, wondering at them all.

FOROBOSCO
Make place, gentlemen; pages, hold torches; the prince approacheth the presence.

DILDO

What squeaking cart-wheel have we here? ha! "Make place, gentlemen; pages, hold torches; the prince approacheth the presence."

ROSSALINE

Faugh, what a strong scent's here! somebody useth to wear socks.

BALURDO

By this fair candle light, 'tis not my feet; I never wore socks since I sucked pap.

ROSSALINE

Savourly put off.

CASTILIO

Hah, her wit stings, blisters, galls off the skin with the tart acrimony of her sharp quickness: by sweetness, she is the very Pallas that flew out of Jupiter's brainpan. Delicious creature, vouchsafe me your service: by the purity of bounty, I shall be proud of such bondage.

ROSSALINE

I vouchsafe it; be my slave.—Signior Balurdo, wilt thou be my servant, too?

BALURDO

O God, forsooth in very good earnest, law, you would make me as a man should say, as a man should say—

FELICHE

'Slud, sweet beauty, will you deign him your service?

ROSSALINE

O, your fool is your only servant. But, good Feliche, why art thou so sad? a penny for thy thought, man.

FELICHE

I sell not my thought so cheap: I value my meditation at a higher rate.

BALURDO

In good sober sadness, sweet mistress, you should have had my thought for a penny: by this crimson satin that cost eleven shillings, thirteen pence, three pence halfpenny a yard, that you should, law!

ROSSALINE

What was thy thought, good servant?

BALURDO

Marry forsooth, how many strike of pease would feed a hog fat against Christtide.

ROSSALINE

Paugh!

[She spits.

Servant, rub out my rheum, it soils the presence.

CASTILIO
By my wealthiest thought, you grace my shoe with an unmeasured honour: I will preserve the sole of it, as a most sacred relic for this service.

ROSSALINE
I'll spit in thy mouth, and thou wilt, to grace thee.

FELICHE [Aside]
O that the stomach of this queasy age
Digests, or brooks such raw unseasoned gobs,
And vomits not them forth! O! slavish sots!
Servant, quoth you? faugh! if a dog should crave
And beg her service, he should have it straight:
She'd give him favours too, to lick her feet,
Or fetch her fan, or some such drudgery:
A good dog's office, which these amorists
Triumph of: 'tis rare, well give her more ass,
More sot, as long as dropping of her nose
Is sworn rich pearl by such low slaves as those.

ROSSALINE
Flavia, attend me to attire me.

[Exeunt **ROSSALINE** and **FLAVIA**.

BALURDO
In sad good earnest, sir, you have touched the very bare of naked truth; my silk stocking hath a good gloss, and I thank my planets, my leg is not altogether unpropitiously shaped. There's a word: unpropitiously? I think I shall speak unpropitiously as well as any courtier in Italy.

FOROBOSCO
So help me your sweet bounty, you have the most graceful presence, applausive elecuty, amazing volubility, polish'd adornation, delicious affability.

FELICHE
Whoop: fut, how he tickles yon trout under the gills! you shall see him take him by and by with groping flattery.

FOROBOSCO
That ever ravish'd the ear of wonder. By your sweet self, than whom I know not a more exquisite, illustrate, accomplished, pure, respected, adored, observed, precious, real, magnanimous, bounteous— if you have an idle rich cast jerkin, or so, it shall not be cast away, if—ha! here's a forehead, an eye, a head, a hair, that would make a—: or if you have any spare pair of silver spurs, I'll do you as much right in all kind offices—

FELICHE [Aside]
Of a kind parasite.

FOROBOSCO
As any of my mean fortunes shall be able to.

BALURDO
As I am true Christian now, thou hast won the spurs.

FELICHE [Aside]
For flattery.
O how I hate that same Egyptian louse,
A rotten maggot, that lives by stinking filth
Of tainted spirits! vengeance to such dogs,
That sprout by gnawing senseless carrion!

[Enter **ALBERTO**.

ALBERTO
Gallants, saw you my mistress, the lady Rossaline?

FOROBOSCO
My mistress, the lady Rossaline, left the presence even now.

CASTILIO
My mistress, the lady Rossaline, withdrew her gracious aspect even now.

BALURDO
My mistress, the lady Rossaline, withdrew her gracious aspect even now.

FELICHE [Aside]
Well said, echo.

ALBERTO
My mistress, and his mistress, and your mistress, and the dog's mistress. Precious dear heaven, that Alberto lives to have such rivals!—
'Slid, I have been searching every private room,
Corner, and secret angle of the court:
And yet, and yet, and yet she lives conceal'd.
Good sweet Feliche, tell me how to find
My bright-faced mistress out.

FELICHE
Why man, cry out for lanthorn and candle-light: for 'tis your only way, to find your bright-flaming wench with your light-burning torch: for most commonly, these light creatures live in darkness.

ALBERTO
Away, you heretic, you'll be burnt for—

FELICHE

Go, you amorous hound, follow the scent of your mistress' shoe; away!

FOROBOSCO

Make a fair presence; boys, advance your lights; the princess makes approach.

BALURDO

And please the gods, now in very good deed, law, you shall see me tickle the measures for the heavens. Do my hangers show?

[Enter **PIERO**, **ANTONIO**, **MELLIDA**, **ROSSALINE**, **GALEATZO**, **MATZAGENTE**, **ALBERTO**, and **FLAVIA**. As they enter, **FELICHE** and **CASTILIO** make a rank for the **DUKE** to pass through. **FOROBOSCO** ushers the **DUKE** to his state: then, whilst **PIERO** speaketh his first speech, **MELLIDA** is taken by **GALEATZO** and **MATZAGENTE** to dance, they supporting her: **ROSSALINE**, in like manner, by **ALBERTO** and **BALURDO**: **FLAVIA**, by **FELICHE** and **CASTILIO**.

PIERO

Beauteous Amazon, sit and seat your thoughts
In the reposure of most soft content.
Sound music there! Nay, daughter, clear your eyes,
From these dull fogs of misty discontent:
Look sprightly, girl. What? though Antonio's drown'd,—
That peevish dotard on thy excellence,
That hated issue of Andrugio,—
Yet may'st thou triumph in my victories;
Since, lo, the high-born bloods of Italy
Sue for thy seat of love.—Let music sound!
Beauty and youth run descant on love's ground.

MATZAGENTE

Lady, erect your gracious symmetry,
Shine in the sphere of sweet affection:
Your eye's as heavy, as the heart of night.

MELLIDA

My thoughts are as black as your beard; my fortunes as ill-proportioned as your legs; and all the powers of my mind as leaden as your wit, and as dusty as your face is swarthy.

GALEATZO

Faith, sweet, I'll lay thee on the lips for that jest.

MELLIDA

I prithee intrude not on a dead man's right.

GALEATZO

No, but the living's just possession:
Thy lips and love are mine.

MELLIDA

You ne'er took seizin on them yet: forbear.
There's not a vacant corner of my heart,
But all is fill'd with dead Antonio's loss.
Then urge no more; O leave to love at all;
'Tis less disgraceful not to mount than fall.

MATZAGENTE

Bright and refulgent lady, deign your ear:
You see this blade,—had it a courtly lip,
It would divulge my valour, plead my love,
Justle that skipping feeble amorist
Out of your love's seat; I am Matzagent.

GALEATZO

Hark thee; I pray thee, taint not thy sweet ear
With that sot's gabble; by thy beauteous cheek,
He is the flagging'st bulrush that e'er droop'd
With each slight mist of rain. But with pleased eye
Smile on my courtship.

MELLIDA

What said you, sir? alas my thought was fix'd
Upon another object. Good, forbear:
I shall but weep. Ay me, what boots a tear!
Come, come, let's dance. O music, thou distill'st
More sweetness in us than this jarring world:
Both time and measure from thy strains do breathe,
Whilst from the channel of this dirt doth flow
Nothing but timeless grief, unmeasured woe.

ANTONIO

O how impatience cramps my crackèd veins
And cruddles thick my blood, with boiling rage!
O eyes, why leap you not like thunderbolts,
Or cannon bullets in my rival's face!
Ohime infeliche misero, O lamentevol fato!

ALBERTO

What means the lady fall upon the ground?

ROSSALINE

Belike the falling sickness.

ANTONIO

I cannot brook this sight, my thoughts grow wild:
Here lies a wretch, on whom heaven never smiled.

ROSSALINE
What, servant, ne'er a word, and I here man?
I would shoot some speech forth, to strike the time
With pleasing touch of amorous compliment.
Say, sweet, what keeps thy mind, what think'st thou on?

ALBERTO
Nothing.

ROSSALINE
What's that nothing?

ALBERTO
A woman's constancy.

ROSSALINE
Good, why, would'st thou have us sluts, and never shift
The vesture of our thoughts? Away for shame.

ALBERTO
O no, th'art too constant to afflict my heart,
Too too firm fixèd in unmovèd scorn.

ROSSALINE
Pish, pish; I fixed in unmovèd scorn!
Why, I'll love thee to-night.

ALBERTO
But whom to-morrow?

ROSSALINE
Faith, as the toy puts me in the head.

BALURDO
And pleased the marble heavens, now would I might be the toy, to put you in the head, kindly to conceit my—my—my—pray you, give in an epithet for love.

FELICHE
Roaring, roaring.

BALURDO
O love, thou hast murder'd me, made me a shadow, and you hear not Balurdo, but Balurdo's ghost.

ROSSALINE
Can a ghost speak?

BALURDO

Scurvily, as I do.

ROSSALINE
And walk?

BALURDO
After their fashion.

ROSSALINE
And eat apples?

BALURDO
In a sort, in their garb.

FELICHE
Prithee, Flavia, be my mistress.

FLAVIA
Your reason, good Feliche?

FELICHE
Faith, I have nineteen mistresses already, and I not much disdain that thou should'st make up the full score.

FLAVIA
O, I hear you make commonplaces of your mistresses to perform the office of memory by. Pray you, in ancient times were not those satin hose? In good faith, now they are new dyed, pink'd, and scoured, they show as well as if they were new. What, mute, Balurdo?

FELICHE
Ay, in faith, and 'twere not for printing, and painting, my breech and your face would be out of reparation.

BALURDO
Ay, in faith, and 'twere not for printing, and painting, my breech and your face would be out of reparation.

FELICHE
Good again, Echo.

FLAVIA
Thou art, by nature, too foul to be affected.

FELICHE
And thou, by art, too fair to be beloved.
By wit's life, most spark spirits, but hard chance.
La ty dine.

PIERO
Gallants, the night grows old; and downy sleep
Courts us to entertain his company:
Our tirèd limbs, bruis'd in the morning fight,
Entreat soft rest, and gentle hush'd repose.
Fill out Greek wines; prepare fresh cressit-light:
We'll have a banquet: Princes, then good-night.

[The cornets sound a senet, and the **DUKE** goes out in state. As they are going out, **ANTONIO** stays **MELLIDA**: the rest exeunt.

ANTONIO
What means these scatter'd looks? why tremble you?
Why quake your thoughts in your distracted eyes?
Collect your spirits, Madam; what do you see?
Dost not behold a ghost?
Look, look where he stalks, wrapt up in clouds of grief,
Darting his soul upon thy wond'ring eyes.
Look, he comes towards thee; see, he stretcheth out
His wretched arms to gird thy loved waist,
With a most wish'd embrace: see'st him not yet?
Nor yet? Ha, Mellida; thou well may'st err:
For look, he walks not like Antonio:
Like that Antonio, that this morning shone
In glistering habiliments of arms,
To seize his love, spite of her father's spite:
But like himself, wretched, and miserable,
Banish'd, forlorn, despairing, strook quite through,
With sinking grief, rolled up in sevenfold doubles
Of plagues unvanquishable: hark, he speaks to thee.

MELLIDA
Alas, I cannot hear, nor see him.

ANTONIO
Why? all this night about the room he stalk'd,
And groan'd, and howl'd, with raging passion,
To view his love (life-blood of all his hopes,
Crown of his fortune) clipp'd by strangers' arms.
Look but behind thee.

MELLIDA
O Antonio!
My lord, my love, my—

ANTONIO
Leave passion, sweet; for time, place, air, and earth,
Are all our foes: fear, and be jealous; fair,

Let's fly.

MELLIDA
Dear heart, ha, whither?

ANTONIO
O, 'tis no matter whither, but let's fly.
Ha! now I think on't, I have ne'er a home,
No father, friend, or country to embrace
These wretched limbs: the world, the all that is,
Is all my foe: a prince not worth a doit:
Only my head is hoisèd to high rate,
Worth twenty thousand double pistolets,
To him that can but strike it from these shoulders.
But come, sweet creature, thou shalt be my home;
My father, country, riches, and my friend,
My all, my soul; and thou and I will live,—
Let's think like what—and you and I will live
Like unmatch'd mirrors of calamity.
The jealous ear of night eave-drops our talk.
Hold thee, there's a jewel; and look thee, there's a note
That will direct thee when, where, how to fly.
Bid me adieu.

MELLIDA
Farewell, bleak misery!

ANTONIO
Stay, sweet, let's kiss before you go!

MELLIDA
Farewell, dear soul!

ANTONIO
Farewell, my life, my heart!

[Exeunt.

ACT III

SCENE I

The sea-shore.

Enter **ANDRUDIO** in armour, **LUCIO** with a shepherd's gown in his hand, and a **PAGE**.

ANDRUGIO

Is not yon gleam the shuddering morn that flakes
With silver tincture the east verge of heaven?

LUCIO

I think it is, so please your excellence.

ANDRUGIO

Away! I have no excellence to please.
Prithee observe the custom of the world,
That only flatters greatness, states exalts.
And please my excellence! O Lucio,
Thou hast been ever held respected dear,
Even precious to Andrugio's inmost love.
Good, flatter not. Nay, if thou giv'st not faith
That I am wretched, O read that, read that.
Piero Sforza to the Italian Princes, fortune.

LUCIO [Reads]

EXCELLENT, the just overthrow Andrugio took in the Venetian gulf, hath so assured the Genoways of the injustice of his cause, and the hatefulness of his person, that they have banish'd him and all his family: and, for confirmation of their peace with us, have vowed, that if he or his son can be attached, to send us both their heads. We therefore, by force of our united league, forbid you to harbour him, or his blood: but if you apprehend his person, we entreat you to send him, or his head, to us. For we vow, by the honour of our blood, to recompense any man that bringeth his head, with twenty thousand double pistolets, and the endearing of our choicest love.
From Venice: Piero Sforza.

ANDRUGIO

My thoughts are fix'd in contemplation
Why this huge earth, this monstrous animal,
That eats her children, should not have eyes and ears.
Philosophy maintains that Nature's wise,
And forms no useless or unperfect thing.
Did Nature make the earth, or the earth Nature?
For earthly dirt makes all things, makes the man,
Moulds me up honour; and, like a cunning Dutchman,
Paints me a puppet even with seeming breath,
And gives a sot appearance of a soul.
Go to, go to; thou liest, Philosophy.
Nature forms things unperfect, useless, vain.
Why made she not the earth with eyes and ears
That she might see desert, and hear men's plaints?
That when a soul is splitted, sunk with grief,
He might fall thus, upon the breast of earth,

[He throws himself on the ground.

Exclaiming thus: O thou all-bearing earth,

Which men do gape for, till thou cramm'st their mouths,
And chokest their throats with dust; O chaune thy breast,
And let me sink into thee! Look who knocks;
Andrugio calls.—But O, she's deaf and blind:
A wretch but lean relief on earth can find.

LUCIO
Sweet lord, abandon passion, and disarm.
Since by the fortune of the tumbling sea,
We are roll'd up upon the Venice marsh,
Let's clip all fortune, lest more low'ring fate—

ANDRUGIO
More low'ring fate! O Lucio, choke that breath.
Now I defy chance: Fortune's brow hath frown'd,
Even to the utmost wrinkle it can bend:
Her venom's spit. Alas, what country rests,
What son, what comfort that she can deprive?
Triumphs not Venice in my overthrow?
Gapes not my native country for my blood?
Lies not my son tomb'd in the swelling main?
And yet more low'ring fate! There's nothing left
Unto Andrugio, but Andrugio:
And that nor mischief, force, distress, nor hell can take.
Fortune my fortunes, not my mind, shall shake.

LUCIO
Spoke like yourself; but give me leave, my Lord,
To wish your safety. If you are but seen,
Your arms display you; therefore put them off,
And take—.

ANDRUGIO
Would'st thou have me go unarm'd among my foes?
Being besieg'd by passion, ent'ring lists,
To combat with despair and mighty grief;
My soul beleaguer'd with the crushing strength
Of sharp impatience? ha, Lucio, go unarm'd?
Come soul, resume the valour of thy birth;
Myself, myself will dare all opposites:
I'll muster forces, an unvanquish'd power:
Cornets of horse shall press th' ungrateful earth;
This hollow wombèd mass shall inly groan,
And murmur to sustain the weight of arms:
Ghastly amazement, with upstarted hair,
Shall hurry on before, and usher us,
Whilst trumpets clamour with a sound of death.

LUCIO

Peace, good my Lord, your speech is all too light.
Alas, survey your fortunes, look what's left
Of all your forces, and your utmost hopes:
A weak old man, a page, and your poor self.

ANDRUGIO

Andrugio lives, and a fair cause of arms,—
Why that's an army all invincible!
He who hath that, hath a battalion royal,
Armour of proof, huge troops of barbèd steeds,
Main squares of pikes, millions of harquebush.
O, a fair cause stands firm, and will abide;
Legions of angels fight upon her side.

LUCIO

Then, noble spirit, slide, in strange disguise,
Unto some gracious Prince, and sojourn there,
Till time and fortune give revenge firm means.

ANDRUGIO

No, I'll not trust the honour of a man.
Gold is grown great, and makes perfidiousness
A common waiter in most princes' courts:
He's in the check-roll; I'll not trust my blood;
I know none breathing but will cog a die
For twenty thousand double pistolets.
How goes the time?

LUCIO

I saw no sun to-day.

ANDRUGIO

No sun will shine, where poor Andrugio breathes.
My soul grows heavy: boy, let's have a song:
We'll sing yet, faith, even in despite of fate.

[A song.

ANDRUGIO

'Tis a good boy, and by my troth, well sung.
O, and thou felt'st my grief, I warrant thee,
Thou would'st have strook division to the height,
And made the life of music breathe: hold, boy; why so.
For God's sake call me not Andrugio,
That I may soon forget what I have been.
For heaven's name, name not Antonio,
That I may not remember he was mine.

Well, ere yon sun set, I'll show myself,
Worthy my blood. I was a Duke; that's all.
No matter whither, but from whence we fall.

[Exeunt.

SCENE II

Palace of the Duke of Venice.

Enter **FELICHE** walking, unbraced.

FELICHE
Castilio, Alberto, Balurdo! none up?
Forobosco! Flattery, nor thou up yet?
Then there's no courtier stirring: that's firm truth?
I cannot sleep: Feliche seldom rests
In these court lodgings. I have walk'd all night,
To see if the nocturnal court delights
Could force me envy their felicity:
And by plain troth, I will confess plain troth,
I envy nothing but the travense light.
O, had it eyes, and ears, and tongues, it might
See sport, hear speech of most strange surquedries.
O, if that candle-light were made a poet,
He would prove a rare firking satirist,
And draw the core forth of imposthum'd sin.
Well, I thank heaven yet, that my content
Can envy nothing, but poor candle-light.
As for the other glistering copper spangs,
That glisten in the tire of the court,
Praise God, I either hate, or pity them.
Well, here I'll sleep till that the scene of up
Is pass'd at court. O calm hush'd rich Content,
Is there a being blessedness without thee?
How soft thou down'st the couch where thou dost rest,
Nectar to life, thou sweet Ambrosian feast!

[Enter **CASTILIO** and his Page **CATZO**: **CASTILIO** with a casting-bottle of sweet water in his hand,
sprinkling himself.

CASTILIO
Am not I a most sweet youth now?

CATZO
Yes, when your throat's perfum'd; your very words

Do smell of ambergris. O stay, sir, stay;
Sprinkle some sweet water to your shoe's heels,
That your mistress may swear you have a sweet foot.

CASTILIO
Good, very good, very passing passing good.

FELICHE
Fut, what treble minikin squeaks there, ha? "good, very good, very very good!"

CASTILIO
I will warble to the delicious conclave of my mistress' ear: and strike her thoughts with the pleasing touch of my voice.

[A song.

CASTILIO
Feliche, health, fortune, mirth, and wine.

FELICHE
To thee, my love divine.

CASTILIO
I drink to thee, sweeting.

FELICHE [Aside]
Plague on thee for an ass!

CASTILIO
Now thou hast seen the court, by the perfection of it, dost not envy it?

FELICHE
I wonder it doth not envy me. Why, man,
I have been borne upon the spirit's wings,
The soul's swift Pegasus, the fantasy:
And from the height of contemplation,
Have view'd the feeble joints men totter on.
I envy none; but hate, or pity all.
For when I view, with an intentive thought,
That creature fair but proud; him rich, but sot;
Th' other witty, but unmeasured arrogant;
Him great, yet boundless in ambition;
Him high-born, but of base life; t' other fear'd,
Yet fearèd fears, and fears most to be loved;
Him wise, but made a fool for public use;
The other learned, but self-opinionate:
When I discourse all these, and see myself
Nor fair, nor rich, nor witty, great, nor fear'd,

Yet amply suited with all full content,
Lord, how I clap my hands, and smooth my brow,
Rubbing my quiet bosom, tossing up
A grateful spirit to Omnipotence!

CASTILIO
Hah, hah! but if thou knew'st my happiness,
Thou would'st even grate away thy soul to dust,
In envy of my sweet beatitude.
I cannot sleep for kisses; I cannot rest
For ladies' letters, that importune me
With such unusèd vehemence of love,
Straight to solicit them, that—.

FELICHE
Confusion seize me, but I think thou liest.
Why should I not be sought to then as well?
Fut, methinks I am as like a man.
Troth, I have a good head of hair, a cheek
Not as yet wan'd, a leg, 'faith, in the full.
I ha' not a red beard, take not tobacco much:
And 'lid, for other parts of manliness—

CASTILIO
Pew waw, you ne'er accourted them in pomp,
Put your good parts in presence graciously.
Ha, and you had, why, they would ha' come off,
Sprung to your arms, and sued, and prayed, and vowed,
And opened all their sweetness to your love.

FELICHE
There are a number of such things as thou
Have often urged me to such loose belief;
But, 'slid, you all do lie, you all do lie.
I have put on good clothes, and smugg'd my face,
Strook a fair wench with a smart, speaking eye;
Courted in all sorts, blunt and passionate;
Had opportunity, put them to the ah!
And, by this light, I find them wondrous chaste,
Impregnable; perchance a kiss, or so:
But for the rest, O most inexorable!

CASTILIO
Nay then, i'faith, prithee look here.

[Shows him the superscription of a seeming letter.

FELICHE

To her most esteemed, loved, and generous servant, Sig. Castilio Balthazar.
Prithee from whom comes this? faith, I must see.
From her that is devoted to thee, in most private sweets of love, Rossaline.
Nay, God's my comfort, I must see the rest;
I must, sans ceremony; faith, I must.

[**FELICHE** takes away the letter by force.

CASTILIO
O, you spoil my ruff, unset my hair; good, away!

FELICHE
Item, for strait canvass, thirteen pence halfpenny; item, for an ell and a half of taffeta to cover your old canvass doublet, fourteen shillings and threepence.—'Slight, this is a tailor's bill.

CASTILIO
In sooth, it is the outside of her letter, on which I took the copy of a tailor's bill.

DILDO
But 'tis not cross'd, I am sure of that. Lord have mercy on him, his credit hath given up the last gasp. Faith, I'll leave him; for he looks as melancholy as a wench the first night she—

[Exit.

FELICHE
Honest musk-cod, 'twill not be so stitched together; take that

[Striking him.

—and that, and belie no lady's love: swear no more by Jesu, this madam, that lady; hence, go, forswear the presence, travel three years to bury this bastinado: avoid, puff-paste, avoid!

CASTILIO
And tell not my lady-mother. Well, as I am a true gentleman, if she had not willed me on her blessing not to spoil my face, if I could not find in my heart to fight, would I might ne'er eat a potato-pie more.

[Exit.

[Enter **BALURDO**, backward; **DILDO** following him with a looking-glass in one hand, and a candle in the other hand: **FLAVIA** following him backward, with a looking-glass in one hand, and a candle in the other; **ROSSALINE** following her; **BALURDO** and **ROSSALINE** stand setting of faces; and so the Scene begins.

FELICHE
More fool, more rare fools! O, for time and place, long enough, and large enough, to act these fools! Here might be made a rare scene of folly, if the plat could bear it.

BALURDO

By the sugar-candy sky, hold up the glass higher, that I may see to swear in fashion. O, one loof more would ha' made them shine; God's neaks, they would have shone like my mistress' brow. Even so the Duke frowns, for all this curson'd world: O, that gern kills, it kills. By my golden—what's the richest thing about me?

DILDO
Your teeth.

BALURDO
By my golden teeth, hold up, that I may put in: hold up, I say, that I may see to put on my gloves.

DILDO
O, delicious, sweet-cheek'd master, if you discharge but one glance from the level of that set face, O, you will strike a wench; you'll make any wench love you.

BALURDO
By Jesu, I think I am as elegant a courtier as—. How likest thou my suit?

CATZO
All, beyond all, no peregal: you are wondered at—
[Aside]
—for an ass.

BALURDO
Well, Dildo, no Christen creature shall know hereafter, what I will do for thee heretofore.

ROSSALINE
Here wants a little white, Flavia.

DILDO
Ay, but, master, you have one little fault; you sleep open-mouth'd.

BALURDO
Pew, thou jest'st. In good sadness, I'll have a looking-glass nail'd to the testern of the bed, that I may see when I sleep whether 'tis so or not; take heed you lie not: go to, take heed you lie not.

FLAVIA
By my troth, you look as like the princess, now—Ay—but her lip is—lip is—a little—redder, a very little redder.

ROSSALINE
But by the help of art or nature, ere I change my periwig, mine shall be as red.

FLAVIA
O ay, that face, that eye, that smile, that writhing of your body, that wanton dandling of your fan, becomes prethely, so sweethly, 'tis even the goodest lady that breathes, the most amiable—. Faith, the fringe of your satin petticoat is ript. Good faith, madam, they say you are the most bounteous lady to your women that ever—most delicious beauty! Good madam, let me kith it.

FELICHE
Rare sport, rare sport! A female fool, and a female flatterer.

ROSSALINE
Body o' me, the Duke! away the glass!

[Enter **PIERO**.

PIERO
Take up your paper, Rossaline.

ROSSALINE
Not mine, my Lord.

PIERO
Not yours, my Lady? I'll see what 'tis.

BALURDO
And how does my sweet mistress? O Lady dear, even as 'tis an old say, "'tis an old horse can neither wighy, nor wag his tail:" even so do I hold my set face still: even so, 'tis a bad courtier that can neither discourse, nor blow his nose.

PIERO [Reads]
Meet me at Abraham's, the Jew's, where I bought my Amazon's disguise. A ship lies in the port, ready bound for England; make haste, come private.   Antonio.

[Enter **CASTILIO** and **FOROBOSCO**.

Forobosco, Alberto, Feliche, Castilio, Balurdo! run, keep the palace, post to the ports, go to my daughter's chamber! whither now? scud to the Jew's! stay, run to the gates, stop the gundolets, let none pass the marsh! do all at once! Antonio! his head, his head! Keep you the court, the rest stand still, or run, or go, or shout, or search, or scud, or call, or hang, or do-do-do su-su-su something! I know not who-who-who what I do-do-do, nor who-who-who, where I am.
O trista traditrice, rea ribalda fortuna,
Negando mi vindetta mi causa fera morte.

[Exeunt **ALL** but **FELICHE**.

FELICHE
Ha ha ha! I could break my spleen at his impatience.

[Enter **ANTONIO** and **MELLIDA**.

ANTONIO
Alma et graziosa fortuna siate favorevole,
Et fortunati siano voti della mia dolce Mellida, Mellida.

MELLIDA
Alas, Antonio, I have lost thy note!
A number mount my stairs; I'll straight return.

[Exit.

FELICHE
Antonio,
Be not affright, sweet Prince; appease thy fear,
Buckle thy spirits up, put all thy wits
In wimble action, or thou art surprised.

ANTONIO
I care not.

FELICHE
Art mad, or desperate? or—

ANTONIO
Both, both, all, all: I prithee let me lie;
Spite of you all, I can, and I will die.

FELICHE
You are distraught; O, this is madness' breath!

ANTONIO
Each man takes hence life, but no man death:
He's a good fellow, and keeps open house:
A thousand thousand ways lead to his gate,
To his wide-mouthèd porch, when niggard life
Hath but one little, little wicket through.
We wring ourselves into this wretched world,
To pule, and weep, exclaim, to curse and rail,
To fret, and ban the fates, to strike the earth,
As I do now. Antonio, curse thy birth,
And die!

FELICHE
Nay, heaven's my comfort, now you are perverse:
You know I always loved you; prithee live.
Wilt thou strike dead thy friends, draw mourning tears?

ANTONIO
Alas, Feliche, I ha' ne'er a friend;
No country, father, brother, kinsman left
To weep my fate or sigh my funeral:
I roll but up and down, and fill a seat
In the dark cave of dusky misery.

FELICHE
'Fore heaven, the Duke comes! hold you, take my key,
Slink to my chamber; look you, that is it:
There shall you find a suit I wore at sea;
Take it, and slip away. Nay, 'precious!
If you'll be peevish, by this light, I'll swear
Thou rail'dst upon thy love before thou diedst,
And call'd her strumpet.

ANTONIO
She'll not credit thee.

FELICHE
Tut, that's all one: I will defame thy love,
And make thy dead trunk held in vile regard.

ANTONIO
Wilt needs have it so? why then, Antonio,
Vive esperanza in dispetto del fato.

[Exit.

[Enter **PIERO**, **GALEATZO**, **MATZAGENTE**, **FOROBOSCO**, **BALURDO**, and **CASTILIO**, with weapons.

PIERO
O, my sweet princes, was't not bravely found?
Even there I found the note, even there it lay:
I kiss the place for joy, that there it lay.
This way he went, here let us make a stand:
I'll keep this gate myself. O gallant youth!
I'll drink carouse unto your country's health
Even in Antonio's skull.

BALURDO
Lord bless us, his breath is more fearful than a sergeant's voice when he cries, I arrest.

[Enter **ANTONIO**, disguised as a sailor.

ANTONIO
Stop Antonio! keep, keep Antonio!

PIERO
Where, where, man, where?

ANTONIO
Here, here: let me pursue him down the marsh!

PIERO
Hold, there's my signet, take a gundelet:
Bring me his head, his head, and, by mine honour,
I'll make thee the wealthiest mariner that breathes.

ANTONIO
I'll sweat my blood out till I have him safe.

PIERO
Spoke heartily, i'faith, good mariner.
O, we will mount in triumph; soon at night,
I'll set his head up. Let's think where.

BALURDO
Upon his shoulders, that's the fittest place for it.
If it be not as fit as if it were made for them, say,—
Balurdo, thou art a sot, an ass.

[Enter **MELLIDA** in Pages attire, dancing.

PIERO
Sprightly, i'faith. In troth he's somewhat like
My daughter Mellida: but, alas! poor soul,
Her honour's heels, God knows, aren't half so light.

MELLIDA [Aside]
Escaped I am, spite of my father's spite.

[Exit.

PIERO
Ho, this will warm my bosom ere I sleep.

[Enter **FLAVIA** running.

FLAVIA
O my Lord, your daughter—

PIERO
Ay, ay, my daughter's safe enough, I warrant thee.—
This vengeance on the boy will lengthen out
My days unmeasuredly.
It shall be chronicled in time to come,
Piero Sforza slew Andrugio's son.

FLAVIA
Ay, but, my Lord, your daughter—

PIERO

Ay, ay, my good wench, she is safe enough.

FLAVIA

O, then, my Lord, you know she's run away.

PIERO

Run away, away! how run away?

FLAVIA

She's vanish'd in an instant, none knows whither.

PIERO

Pursue, pursue, fly, run, post, scud away!

FELICHE [Sings]

"And was not good king Salomon," &c.

PIERO

Fly, call, run, row, ride, cry, shout, hurry, haste!
Haste, hurry, shout, cry, ride, row, run, call, fly,
Backward and forward, every way about!
Male detta fortuna che dura sorte!
Che farò, che dirò, pur fugir tanto mal!

CASTILIO

'Twas you that struck me even now: was it not?

FELICHE

It was I that struck you even now.

CASTILIO

You bastinadoed me, I take it.

FELICHE

I bastinadoed you, and you took it.

CASTILIO

'Faith, sir, I have the richest tobacco in the court for you; I would be glad to make you satisfaction, if I have wronged you. I would not the sun should set upon your anger; give me your hand.

FELICHE

Content, faith; so thou'lt breed no more such lies.
I hate not man, but man's lewd qualities.

[Exeunt.

ACT IV

SCENE I

Sea-shore near Venice.

Enter **ANTONIO**, in his sea-gown running.

ANTONIO
Stop, stop Antonio, stay Antonio!
Vain breath, vain breath, Antonio's lost;
He cannot find himself, not seize himself.
Alas, this that you see is not Antonio;
His spirit hovers in Piero's court,
Hurling about his agile faculties,
To apprehend the sight of Mellida:
But poor, poor soul, wanting apt instruments
To speak or see, stands dumb and blind, sad spirit,
Roll'd up in gloomy clouds as black as air
Through which the rusty coach of Night is drawn.
'Tis so; I'll give you instance that 'tis so.
Conceit you me: as having clasp'd a rose
Within my palm, the rose being ta'en away,
My hand retains a little breath of sweet:
So may man's trunk, his spirit slipp'd away,
Hold still a faint perfume of his sweet guest.
'Tis so; for when discursive powers fly out,
And roam in progress through the bounds of heaven,
The soul itself gallops along with them,
As chieftain of this wingèd troop of thought,
Whilst the dull lodge of spirit standeth waste,
Until the soul return from—. What was't I said?
O, this is naught but speckling melancholy.
I have been—
That Morpheus' tender skinp—Cousin german
Bear with me, good—
Mellida: clod upon clod thus fall.
Hell is beneath, yet heaven is over all.

[Falls on the ground.

[Enter **ANDRUGIO**, **LUCIO**, and **PAGE**.

ANDRUGIO
Come, Lucio, let's go eat: what hast thou got?
Roots, roots? alas, they are seeded, new cut up.
O, thou hast wrongèd Nature, Lucio:

But boots not much; thou but pursu'st the world,
That cuts off virtue, 'fore it comes to growth,
Lest it should seed, and so o'errun her son,
Dull purblind error.—Give me water, boy.
There is no poison in't, I hope; they say
That lurks in massy plate: and yet the earth
Is so infected with a general plague,
That he's most wise, that thinks there's no man fool;
Right prudent, that esteems no creature just;
Great policy the least things to mistrust.
Give me assay—. How we mock greatness now!

LUCIO
A strong conceit is rich, so most men deem;
If not to be, 'tis comfort yet to seem.

ANDRUGIO
Why man, I never was a prince till now.
'Tis not the barèd pate, the bended knees,
Gilt tipstaves, Tyrrian purple, chairs of state,
Troops of pied butterflies that flutter still
In greatness' summer, that confirm a prince:
'Tis not the unsavoury breath of multitudes,
Shouting and clapping, with confusèd din,
That makes a prince. No, Lucio, he's a king,
A true right king, that dares do aught save wrong;
Fears nothing mortal but to be unjust;
Who is not blown up with the flattering puffs
Of spongy sycophants; who stands unmov'd,
Despite the justling of opinion;
Who can enjoy himself, maugre the throng
That strive to press his quiet out of him;
Who sits upon Jove's footstool, as I do,
Adoring, not affecting, majesty;
Whose brow is wreathèd with the silver crown
Of clear content: this, Lucio, is a king,
And of this empire every man's possest
That's worth his soul.

LUCIO
My Lord, the Genoways had wont to say—

ANDRUGIO
Name not the Genoways: that very word
Unkings me quite, makes me vile passion's slave.
O, you that slide upon the glibbery ice
Of vulgar favour, view Andrugio.
Was never prince with more applause confirm'd,

With louder shouts of triumph launchèd out
Into the surgy main of government;
Was never prince with more despite cast out,
Left shipwrack'd, banish'd, on more guiltless ground.
O rotten props of the crazed multitude,
How you still double, falter under the lightest chance
That strains your veins! Alas, one battle lost,
Your whorish love, your drunken healths, your houts and shouts,
Your smooth God save's, and all your devils lost
That tempts our quiet to your hell of throngs!
Spit on me, Lucio, for I am turnèd slave:
Observe how passion domineers o'er me.

LUCIO
No wonder, noble Lord, having lost a son,
A country, crown, and—.

ANDRUGIO
Ay, Lucio, having lost a son, a son,
A country, house, crown, son. O lares, miseri lares!
Which shall I first deplore? My son, my son,
My dear sweet boy, my dear Antonio!

ANTONIO
Antonio?

ANDRUGIO
Ay, echo, ay; I mean Antonio.

ANTONIO
Antonio, who means Antonio?

ANDRUGIO
Where art? what art? know'st thou Antonio?

ANTONIO
Yes.

ANDRUGIO
Lives he?

ANTONIO
No.

ANDRUGIO
Where lies he dead?

ANTONIO

Here.

ANDRUGIO
Where?

ANTONIO
Here.

ANDRUGIO
Art thou Antonio?

ANTONIO
I think I am.

ANDRUGIO
Dost thou but think? What, dost not know thyself?

ANTONIO
He is a fool that thinks he knows himself.

ANDRUGIO
Upon thy faith to heaven, give thy name.

ANTONIO
I were not worthy of Andrugio's blood,
If I denied my name's Antonio.

ANDRUGIO
I were not worthy to be call'd thy father,
If I denied my name Andrugio.
And dost thou live? O, let me kiss thy cheek,
And dew thy brow with trickling drops of joy.
Now heaven's will be done: for I have lived
To see my joy, my son Antonio.
Give me thy hand; now fortune do thy worst,
His blood, that lapp'd thy spirit in the womb,
Thus (in his love) will make his arms thy tomb.

ANTONIO
Bless not the body with your twining arms,
Which is accurs'd of heaven. O, what black sin
Hath been committed by our ancient house,
Whose scalding vengeance lights upon our heads,
That thus the world and fortune casts us out,
As loathèd objects, ruin's branded slaves!

ANDRUGIO
Do not expostulate the heavens' will,

But, O, remember to forget thyself;
Forget remembrance what thou once hast been.
Come, creep with me from out this open air:
Even trees have tongues, and will betray our life.
I am a-raising of our house, my boy,
Which fortune will not envy, 'tis so mean,
And like the world (all dirt): there shalt thou rip
The inwards of thy fortunes in mine ears,
While I sit weeping, blind with passion's tears.
Then I'll begin, and we'll such order keep,
That one shall still tell griefs, the other weep.

[Exeunt **ANDRUGIO** and **LUCIO**, leaving **ANTONIO** and the **PAGE**.

ANTONIO
I'll follow you. Boy, prithee stay a little.
Thou hast had a good voice, if this cold marsh
Wherein we lurk have not corrupted it.

[Enter **MELLIDA**, standing out of sight, in her Page's suit.

I prithee sing, but, sirra, (mark you me)
Let each note breathe the heart of passion,
The sad extracture of extremest grief.
Make me a strain speak groaning like a bell
That tolls departing souls;
Breathe me a point that may enforce me weep,
To wring my hands, to break my cursèd breast,
Rave, and exclaim, lie grovelling on the earth,
Straight start up frantic, crying, Mellida!
Sing but, Antonio hath lost Mellida,
And thou shalt see me (like a man possess'd)
Howl out such passion, that even this brinish marsh
Will squeeze out tears from out his spongy cheeks:
The rocks even groan, and—prithee, prithee sing,
Or I shall ne'er ha' done when I am in;
'Tis harder for me end, than to begin.

[The **BOY** runs a note, **ANTONIO** breaks it.

For look thee, boy, my grief that hath no end,
I may begin to plain, but—prithee, sing.

[A song.

MELLIDA
Heaven keep you, sir!

ANTONIO
Heaven keep you from me, sir!

MELLIDA
I must be acquainted with you, sir.

ANTONIO
Wherefore? Art thou infected with misery,
Sear'd with the anguish of calamity?
Art thou true sorrow, hearty grief? canst weep?
I am not for thee if thou canst not rave,

[**ANTONIO** falls on the ground.

Fall flat on the ground, and thus exclaim on heaven:
O trifling nature, why inspired'st thou breath?

MELLIDA
Stay, sir, I think you namèd Mellida.

ANTONIO
Know'st thou Mellida?

MELLIDA
Yes.

ANTONIO
Hast thou seen Mellida?

MELLIDA
Yes.

ANTONIO
Then hast thou seen the glory of her sex,
The music of Nature, the unequall'd lustre
Of unmatch'd excellence, the united sweet
Of heaven's graces, the most adorèd beauty,
That ever strook amazement in the world!

MELLIDA
You seem to love her.

ANTONIO
With my very soul.

MELLIDA
She'll not requite it: all her love is fix'd
Upon a gallant, one Antonio,

The Duke of Genoa's son. I was her page,
And often as I waited, she would sigh,
O, dear Antonio! and to strengthen thought,
Would clip my neck, and kiss, and kiss me thus.
Therefore leave loving her: fa, faith methinks
Her beauty is not half so ravishing
As you discourse of; she hath a freckled face,
A low forehead, and a lumpish eye.

ANTONIO
O heaven, that I should hear such blasphemy!
Boy, rogue, thou liest! and
Spavento del mio cor dolce Mellida,
Di grave morte ristoro vero, dolce Mellida,
Celeste salvatrice, sovrana Mellida
Del mio sperar; trofeo vero Mellida.

MELLIDA
Diletta e soave anima mia Antonio,
Godevole bellezza cortese Antonio.
Signior mio e virginal amore bell'Antonio,
Gusto delli miei sensi, car'Antonio.

ANTONIO
O svanisce il cor in un soave bacio.

MELLIDA
Muoiono i sensi nel desiato desio:

ANTONIO
Nel cielo può esser beltà più chiara?

MELLIDA
Nel mondo può esser beltà più chiara?

ANTONIO
Dammi un bacio da quella bocca beata,
Lasciami coglier l'aura odorata
Che ha sua seggia in quelle dolci labbra.

MELLIDA
Dammi per impero del tuo gradit'amore
Che bea me con sempiterno honore,
Così, così mi converrà morir.
Good sweet, scout o'er the marsh, for my heart trembles
At every little breath that strikes my ear.
When thou returnest, then I will discourse
How I deceiv'd the court; then thou shalt tell

How thou escaped'st the watch: we'll point our speech
With amorous kissing commas, and even suck
The liquid breath from out each other's lips.

ANTONIO
Dull clod, no man but such sweet favour clips.
I go, and yet my panting blood persuades me stay.
Turn coward in her sight? away, away!

[Exit.

PAGE
I think confusion of Babel is fall'n upon those lovers, that they change their language; but I fear me, my master having but feigned the person of a woman, hath got their unfeigned imperfection, and is grown double tongued: as for Mellida, she were no woman, if she could not yield strange language. But howsoever, if I should sit in judgment, 'tis an error easier to be pardoned by the auditors, than excused by the authors; and yet some private respect may rebate the edge of the keener censure.

[Enter **PIERO, CASTILIO, MATZAGENTE, FOROBOSCO, FELICHE, GALEATZO**, at one door; **BALURDO**, and his **PAGE**, at another door.

PIERO
This way she took: search, my sweet gentlemen.
How now, Balurdo, canst thou meet with anybody?

BALURDO
As I am true gentleman, I made my horse sweat, that he hath ne'er a dry thread on him: and I can meet with no living creature, but men and beasts. In good sadness, I would have sworn I had seen Mellida even now; for I saw a thing stir under a hedge, and I peep'd, and I spied a thing, and I peer'd, and I tweer'd underneath: and truly a right wise man might have been deceived, for it was—.

PIERO
What, in the name of heaven?

BALURDO
A dun cow.

FELICHE
Sh'ad ne'er a kettle on her head?

PIERO
Boy, did'st thou see a young lady pass this way?

GALEATZO
Why speak you not?

BALURDO
God's neaks, proud elf, give the Duke reverence!

Stand bare with a—.
Whogh! heavens bless me! Mellida, Mellida!

PIERO
Where man, where?

BALURDO
Turned man, turned man; women wear the breeches.
Lo, here!

PIERO
Light and unduteous! kneel not, peevish elf;
Speak not, entreat not, shame unto my house,
Curse to my honour. Where's Antonio?
Thou traitress to my hate, what, is he shipp'd
For England now? well, whimpering harlot, hence!

MELLIDA
Good father!

PIERO
Good me no goods. Seest thou that sprightly youth?
Ere thou canst term to-morrow morning old,
Thou shalt call him thy husband, lord, and love.

MELLIDA
Ay me!

PIERO
Blirt on your "ay me's!" guard her safely hence.
Drag her away, I'll be your guard to-night.
Young prince, mount up your spirits and prepare
To solemnise your nuptial's eve with pomp.

GALEATZO
The time is scant: now nimble wits appear:
Phœbus begins to gleam, the welkin's clear.

[Exeunt all but **BALURDO** and his **PAGE**.

BALURDO
Now nimble wits appear! I'll myself appear,
Balurdo's self, that in quick wit doth surpass,
Will show the substance of a complete—.

DILDO
Ass, ass.

BALURDO

I'll mount my courser, and most gallantly prick—.

DILDO

Gallantly prick is too long, and stands hardly in the verse, sir.

BALURDO

I'll speak pure rhyme, and will so bravely prank it, that I'll toss love like a—prank, prank it!—a rhyme for prank it?

DILDO

Blanket.

BALURDO

That I'll toss love, like a dog in a blanket. Hah hah, indeed, law. I think, hah hah; I think, hah hah, I think I shall tickle the Muses. And I strike it not dead, say, Balurdo, thou art an arrant sot.

DILDO

Balurdo, thou art an arrant sot.

[Enter **ANDRUGIO** and **ANTONIO** wreathed together, **LUCIO**.

ANDRUGIO

Now, come, united force of chap-fall'n death;
Come, power of fretting anguish, leave distress.
O, thus enfolded, we have breasts of proof
'Gainst all the venom'd stings of misery.

ANTONIO

Father, now I have an antidote
'Gainst all the poison that the world can breathe:
My Mellida, my Mellida doth bless
This bleak waste with her presence.—How now, boy,
Why dost thou weep? alas! where's Mellida?

PAGE

Ay me, my Lord.

ANTONIO

A sudden horror doth invade my blood;
My sinews tremble, and my panting heart
Scuds round about my bosom, to go out,
Dreading the assailant, horrid passion.
O, be no tyrant, kill me with one blow;
Speak quickly, briefly, boy.

PAGE

Her father found, and seized her; she is gone.

ANDRUGIO

Son, heat thy blood, be not froze up with grief
Courage, sweet boy, sink not beneath the weight
Of crushing mischief. O where's thy dauntless heart,
Thy father's spirit! I renounce thy blood,
If thou forsake thy valour.

LUCIO

See how his grief speaks in his slow-paced steps.
Alas!
'Tis more than he can utter, let him go:
Dumb solitary path best suiteth woe.

[Exit **ANTONIO**.

ANDRUGIO

Give me my arms, my armour, Lucio.

LUCIO

Dear lord, what means this rage? when lacking use
Scarce safe's your life, will you in armour rise?

ANDRUGIO

Fortune fears valour, presseth cowardice.

LUCIO

Then valour gets applause, when it hath place,
And means to blaze it.

ANDRUGIO

Nunquam potest non esse.

LUCIO

Patience, my lord, may bring your ills some end.

ANDRUGIO

What patience, friend, can ruin'd hopes attend?
Come, let me die like old Andrugio,
Worthy my birth. O, blood-true-honour'd graves
Are far more blessèd than base life of slaves.

[Exeunt.

Palace of the Duke of Venice.

Enter **BALURDO**, a **PAINTER** with two pictures, and **DILDO**.

BALURDO
And are you a painter? sir, can you draw, can you draw?

PAINTER
Yes, sir.

BALURDO
Indeed, law! now so can my father's forehorse. And are these the workmanship of your hands?

PAINTER
I did limn them.

BALURDO
Limn them? a good word, limn them: whose picture is this? Anno Domini, 1599. Believe me, master Anno Domini was of a good settled age when you limn'd him: 1599 years old! Let's see the other. Ætatis suæ. Byrlady, he is somewhat younger. Belike master Ætatis suæ was Anno Domini's son.

PAINTER
Is not your master a—

DILDO
He hath a little proclivity to him.

PAINTER
Proclivity, good youth? I thank you for your courtly proclivity.

BALURDO
Approach, good sir. I did send for you to draw me a device, an Imprezza, by Synecdoche a Mott. By Phœbus' crimson taffeta mantle, I think I speak as melodiously,—look you, sir, how think you on't? I would have you paint me, for my device, a good fat leg of ewe mutton, swimming in stewed broth of plums (boy, keel your mouth, it runs over) and the word shall be, Hold my dish, whilst I spill my pottage. Sure, in my conscience, 'twould be the most sweet device, now.

PAINTER
'Twould scent of kitchen-stuff too much.

BALURDO
God's neaks, now I remember me, I ha' the rarest device in my head that ever breathed. Can you paint me a driveling reeling song, and let the word be, Uh.

PAINTER
A belch?

BALURDO

O, no no: Uh, paint me Uh, or nothing.

PAINTER

It cannot be done, sir, but by a seeming kind of drunkenness.

BALURDO

No? well, let me have a good massy ring, with your own posy graven in it, that must sing a small treble, word for word, thus:
And if you will my true lover be,
Come follow me to the green wood.

PAINTER

O Lord, sir, I cannot make a picture sing.

BALURDO

Why? 'slid, I have seen painted things sing as sweet;
But I have't will tickle it for a conceit, i'faith.

[Enter **FELICHE** and **ALBERTO**.

ALBERTO

O dear Feliche, give me thy device.
How shall I purchase love of Rossaline?

FELICHE

'Swill, flatter her soundly.

ALBERTO

Her love is such, I cannot flatter her:
But with my utmost vehemence of speech,
I have ador'd her beauties.

FELICHE

Hast writ good moving unaffected rhymes to her?

ALBERTO

O, yes, Feliche, but she scorns my writ.

FELICHE

Hast thou presented her with sumptuous gifts?

ALBERTO

Alas, my fortunes are too weak to offer them.

FELICHE

O, then I have it, I'll tell thee what to do.

ALBERTO
What, good Feliche?

FELICHE
Go and hang thyself; I say, go hang thyself,
If that thou canst not give, go hang thyself:
I'll rhyme thee dead, or verse thee to the rope.
How think'st thou of a poet that sung thus?
Munera sola pacant, sola addunt munera formam:
Munere sollicites Pallada, Cypris erit.
Munera, munera!

ALBERTO
I'll go and breathe my woes unto the rocks,
And spend my grief upon the deafest seas.
I'll weep my passion to the senseless trees,
And load most solitary air with plaints.
For woods, trees, sea, or rocky Apennine,
Is not so ruthless as my Rossaline.
Farewell, dear friend, expect no more of me:
Here ends my part in this love's comedy.

[Exeunt **ALBERTO** and **PAINTER**.

FELICHE
Now, master Balurdo, whither are you going, ha?

BALURDO
Signior Feliche, how do you, faith? and by my troth, how do you?

FELICHE
Whither art thou going, bully?

BALURDO
And as heaven help me, how do you?
How, do you, i'faith, hee?

FELICHE
Whither art going, man?

BALURDO
O God, to the court; I'll be willing to give you grace and good countenance, if I may but see you in the presence.

FELICHE
O, to court? farewell.

BALURDO

If you see one in a yellow taffeta doublet, cut upon carnation velure, a green hat, a blue pair of velvet hose, a gilt rapier, and an orange-tawny pair of worsted silk stockings, that's I, that's I.

FELICHE

Very good: farewell.

BALURDO

Ho, you shall know me as easily; I ha' bought me a new green feather with a red sprig; you shall see my wrought shirt hang out at my breeches; you shall know me.

FELICHE

Very good, very good, farewell.

BALURDO

Marry, in the mask 'twill be somewhat hard. But if you hear anybody speak so wittily, that he makes all the room laugh; that's I, that's I. Farewell, good Signior.

[Enter **FOROBOSCO**, **CASTILIO**, a **BOY** carrying a gilt harp; **PIERO**, **MELLIDA**, in night apparel; **ROSSALINE**, **FLAVIA**, **TWO PAGES**.

PIERO

Advance the music's prize; now, cap'ring wits,
Rise to your highest mount; let choice delight
Garland the brow of this triumphant night.
'Sfoot, 'a sits like Lucifer himself.

ROSSALINE

Good sweet Duke,
First let their voices strain for music's prize.
Give me the golden harp:
Faith, with your favour, I'll be umperess.

PIERO

Sweet niece, content: boys, clear your voice and sing.

[**FIRST BOY** sings.

ROSSALINE

By this gold, I had rather have a servant with a short nose, and a thin hair, than have such a high-stretch'd minikin voice.

PIERO

Fair niece, your reason?

ROSSALINE

By the sweet of love, I should fear extremely that he were an eunuch.

CASTILIO
Spark spirit, how like you his voice?

ROSSALINE
Spark spirit, how like you his voice!
So help me, youth, thy voice squeaks like a dry corkshoe: come, come; let's hear the next.

[**SECOND BOY** sings.

PIERO
Trust me, a strong mean. Well sung, my boy.

[Enter **BALRUDO**.

BALURDO
Hold, hold, hold: are ye blind? could ye not see my voice coming for the harp? And I knock not division on the head, take hence the harp, make me a slip, and let me go but for ninepence. Sir Mark, strike up for master Balurdo.

[**THIRD BOY** sings.

Judgment, gentlemen, judgment! Was't not above line?
I appeal to your mouths that heard my song.
Do me right, and dub me knight, Balurdo.

ROSSALINE
Kneel down, and I'll dub thee knight of the golden harp.

BALURDO
Indeed, law, do, and I'll make you lady of the silver fiddlestick.

ROSSALINE
Come, kneel, kneel.

[Enter a **PAGE** to **BALURDO**.

BALURDO
My troth, I thank you, it hath never a whistle in't.

ROSSALINE
Nay, good sweet coz, raise up your drooping eyes; and I were at the point of To have and to hold from this day forward, I would be asham'd to look thus lumpish. What, my pretty coz, 'tis but the loss of an odd maidenhead.
Shall's dance? thou art so sad, hark in thine ear:
I was about to say, but I'll forbear.

BALURDO

I come, I come; more than most honeysuckle sweet ladies, pine not for my presence, I'll return in pomp. Well spoke, Sir Jeffrey Balurdo. As I am a true knight, I feel honourable eloquence begin to grope me already.

[Exit.

PIERO
Faith, mad niece, I wonder when thou wilt marry?

ROSSALINE
Faith, kind uncle, when men abandon jealousy, forsake taking of tobacco, and cease to wear their beards so rudely long. O, to have a husband with a mouth continually smoking, with a bush of furze on the ridge of his chin, ready still to flop into his foaming chaps; ah, 'tis more than most intolerable.

PIERO
Nay faith, sweet niece, I was mighty strong in thought we should have shut up night with an old comedy: the Prince of Florence shall have Mellida, and thou should'st have—.

ROSSALINE
Nobody, good sweet uncle. I tell you, sir, I have thirty-nine servants, and my monkey that makes the fortieth. Now I love all of them lightly for something, but affect none of them seriously for anything. One's a passionate fool, and he flatters me above belief; the second's a testy ape, and he rails at me beyond reason; the third's as grave as some censor, and he strokes up his mustachios three times, and makes six plots of set faces, before he speaks one wise word; the fourth's as dry as the bur of an hartichoke; the fifth paints, and hath always a good colour for what he speaks; the sixth—.

PIERO
Stay, stay, sweet niece, what makes you thus suspect your gallants' worth?

ROSSALINE
O, when I see one wear a periwig, I dread his hair; another wallow in a great slop, I mistrust the proportion of his thigh; and wears a ruffled boot, I fear the fashion of his leg. Thus, something in each thing, one trick in everything makes me mistrust imperfection in all parts; and there's the full point of my addiction.

[The cornets sound a senet. Enter **GALEATZO**, **MATZAGENTE**, and **BALURDO** in maskery.

PIERO
The room's too scant: boys, stand in there, close.

MELLIDA [To **GALEATZO**]
In faith, fair sir, I am too sad to dance.

PIERO
How's that, how's that? too sad? By heaven, dance,
And grace him too, or go to—, I say no more.

MELLIDA

A burning glass, the word splendente Phœbo?
It is too curious, I conceit it not.

GALEATZO
Faith, I'll tell thee. I'll no longer burn,
Than you will shine and smile upon my love.
For look ye, fairest, by your pure sweets,
I do not dote upon your excellence;
And faith, unless you shed your brightest beams
Of sunny favour and acceptive grace
Upon my tender love, I do not burn:
Marry, but shine, and I'll reflect your beams
With fervent ardour. Faith! I would be loath to flatter thee, fair soul, because I love, not dote, court like thy husband, which thy father swears to-morrow morn I must be. This is all; and now from henceforth, trust me, Mellida, I'll not speak one wise word to thee more.

MELLIDA
I trust ye.

GALEATZO
By my troth, I'll speak pure fool to thee now.

MELLIDA
You will speak the liker yourself.

GALEATZO
Good faith, I'll accept of the coxcomb, so you will not refuse the bable.

MELLIDA
Nay, good sweet, keep them both; I am enamoured of neither.

GALEATZO
Go to, I must take you down for this. Lend me your ear.

ROSSALINE
A glow-worm? the word,—Splendescit tantùm tenebris.

MATZAGENTE
O, lady, the glow-worm figurates my valour, which shineth brightest in most dark, dismal, and horrid achievements.

ROSSALINE
Or rather, your glow-worm represents your wit, which only seems to have fire in it, though indeed 'tis but an ignis fatuus, and shines only in the dark dead night of fools' admiration.

MATZAGENTE
Lady, my wit hath spurs, if it were dispos'd to ride you.

ROSSALINE
Faith, sir, your wit's spurs have but walking rowels; dull, blunt, they will not draw blood: the gentlemen-ushers may admit them the presence, for any wrong they can do to ladies.

BALURDO
Truly, I have strained a note above ela for a device: look you, 'tis a fair-ruled singing book; the word, Perfect, if it were prick'd.

FLAVIA
Though you are mask'd, I can guess who you are by your wit. You are not the exquisite Balurdo, the most rarely-shaped Balurdo.

BALURDO
Who, I? No, I am not Sir Jeffrey Balurdo. I am not as well known by my wit as an alehouse by a red lattice. I am not worthy to love and be beloved of Flavia.

FLAVIA
I will not scorn to favour such good parts As are applauded in your rarest self.

BALURDO
Truly, you speak wisely, and like a jantlewoman of fourteen years of age. You know the stone called lapis; the nearer it comes to the fire, the hotter it is: and the bird, which the geometricians call avis, the farther it is from the earth, the nearer it is to the heaven; and love, the nigher it is to the flame, the more remote (there's a word, remote!) the more remote it is from the frost. Your wit is quick; a little thing pleaseth a young lady, and a small favour contenteth an old courtier; and so, sweet mistress, I truss my codpiece point.

[Enter **FELICHE**.

PIERO
What might import this flourish? Bring us word.

FELICHE
Stand away: here's such a company of flyboats, hulling about this galleasse of greatness, that there's no boarding him.
Do you hear, yon thing call'd duke?

PIERO
How now, blunt Feliche; what's the news?

FELICHE
Yonder's a knight, hath brought Andrugio's head,
And craves admittance to your chair of state.

[Cornets sound a senet. Enter **ANDRUGIO** in armour.

PIERO
Conduct him with attendance sumptuous;

Sound all the pleasing instruments of joy;
Make triumph stand on tiptoe whilst we meet:
O sight most gracious, O revenge most sweet!

ANDRUGIO

We vow, by the honour of our birth, to recompense any man that bringeth Andrugio's head, with twenty thousand double pistolets, and the endearing to our choicest love.

PIERO

We still with most unmoved resolve confirm
Our large munificence, and here breathe
A sad and solemn protestation:
When I recall this vow, O, let our house
Be even commanded, stain'd, and trampled on,
As worthless rubbish of nobility.

ANDRUGIO

Then here
[Raising his beaver]
—Piero, is Andrugio's head,
Royally casquèd in a helm of steel:
Give me thy love, and take it. My dauntless soul
Hath that unbounded vigour in his spirits
That it can bear more rank indignity,
With less impatience than thy canker'd hate
Can sting and venom his untainted worth
With the most vip'rous sound of malice. Strike!
O, let no glimpse of honour light thy thoughts;
If there be any heat of royal breath
Creeping in thy veins, O stifle it;
Be still thyself, bloody and treacherous.
Fame not thy house with an admirèd act
Of princely pity. Piero, I am come
To soil thy house with an eternal blot
Of savage cruelty; strike, or bid me strike.
I pray my death; that thy ne'er-dying shame
Might live immortal to posterity.
Come, be a princely hangman, stop my breath.
O dread thou shame, no more than I dread death.

PIERO

We are amazed, our royal spirit's numb'd
In stiff astonish'd wonder at thy prowess.
Most mighty, valiant, and high-tow'ring heart,
We blush, and turn our hate upon ourselves,
For hating such an unpeer'd excellence.
I joy my state: him whom I loath'd before,
That now I honour, love, nay more, adore.

[The still flutes sound a mournful senet. Enter a funeral **PROCESSION**, followed by **LUCIO**.

But stay; what tragic spectacle appears!
Whose body bear you in that mournful hearse?

LUCIO
The breathless trunk of young Antonio.

MELLIDA
Antonio! ay me! my lord, my love! my—.

ANDRUGIO
Sweet precious issue of most honour'd blood,
Rich hope, ripe virtue, O untimely loss!
Come hither, friend: prithee, do not weep.
Why, I am glad he's dead; he shall not see
His father's vanquish'd by his enemy,
Even in princely honour. Nay, prithee, speak!
How died the wretched boy?

LUCIO
My lord!

ANDRUGIO
I hope he died yet like my son, i'faith.

LUCIO
Alas, my lord!

ANDRUGIO
He died unforced, I trust, and valiantly?

LUCIO
Poor gentleman, being—

ANDRUGIO
Did his hand shake, or his eye look dull,
His thoughts reel fearful when he struck the stroke?
And if they did, I'll rend them out the hearse,
Rip up his cerecloth, mangle his bleak face,
That when he comes to heaven, the powers divine,
Shall ne'er take notice that he was my son:
I'll quite disclaim his birth. Nay, prithee, speak!
And 'twere not hooped with steel, my breast would break.

MELLIDA
O that my spirit in a sigh could mount

Into the sphere where thy sweet soul doth rest!

PIERO
O that my tears, bedewing thy wan cheek,
Could make new spirit sprout in thy cold blood!

BALURDO
Verily, he looks as pitifully as a poor John; as I am true knight, I could weep like a ston'd horse.

ANDRUGIO
Villain, 'tis thou hast murderèd my son!
Thy unrelenting spirit, thou black dog,
That took'st no passion of his fatal love,
Hath forced him give his life untimely end.

PIERO
O! that my life, her love, my dearest blood,
Would but redeem one minute of his breath!

ANTONIO [Rising]
I seize that breath. Stand not amazed, great states;
I rise from death that never lived till now.
Piero, keep thy vow, and I enjoy
More unexpressèd height of happiness
Than power of thought can reach; if not, lo, here
There stands my tomb, and here a pleasing stage.
Most-wish'd spectators of my tragedy,
To this end have I feign'd, that her fair eye,
For whom I lived, might bless me ere I die.

MELLIDA
Can breath depaint my unconceivèd thoughts?
Can words describe my infinite delight
Of seeing thee, my lord Antonio?
O no; conceit, breath, passion, words, be dumb,
Whilst I instill the dew of my sweet bliss,
In the soft pressure of a melting kiss!
Sic, sic juvat ire sub umbras.

PIERO
Fair son (now I'll be proud to call thee son),
Enjoy me thus: my very breast is thine;
Possess me freely, I am wholly thine.

ANTONIO
Dear father—

ANDRUGIO

Sweet son, sweet son, I can speak no more:
My joy's passion flows above the shore,
And chokes the current of my speech.

PIERO
Young Florence prince, to you my lips must beg
For a remittance of your interest.

GALEATZO
In your fair daughter? with all my thought.
So help me faith, the nak'd truth I'll unfold;
He that was never hot will soon be cold.

PIERO
No man else makes claim unto her?

MATZAGENTE
The valiant speak truth in brief: no—

BALURDO
Truly, for Sir Jeffrey Balurdo, he disclaims to have had anything in her.

PIERO
Then here I give her to Antonio.
Royal, valiant, most respected prince,
Let's clip our hands, I'll thus observe my vow:
I promised twenty thousand double pistolets,
With the endearing to my dearest love,
To him that brought thy head; thine be the gold,
To solemnise our houses' unity;
My love be thine, the all I have, be thine.
Fill us fresh wine, the form we'll take by this;
We'll drink a health, while they two sip a kiss.
Now there remains no discord that can sound
Harsh accents to the ear of our accord:
So please you, niece, to match.

ROSSALINE
Troth, uncle, when my sweet-faced coz hath told me how she likes the thing called wedlock, may be I'll take a survey of the checkroll of my servants; and he that hath the best parts of—I'll prick him down for my husband.

BALURDO
For passion of love now, remember me to my mistress, lady Rossaline, when she is pricking down the good parts of her servants. As I am true knight, I grow stiff; I shall carry it.

PIERO
I will.

Sound Lydian wires, once make a pleasing note
On nectar streams of your sweet airs to float.

ANTONIO
Here ends the comic crosses of true love;
O! may the passage most successful prove!

ANDRUGIO
Gentlemen, though I remain an armed Epilogue, I stand not as a peremptory challenger of desert, either for him that composed the Comedy, or for us that acted it; but a most submissive suppliant for both. What imperfection you have seen in us, leave with us, and we'll amend it; what hath pleased you, take with you, and cherish it. You shall not be more ready to embrace anything commendable, than we will endeavour to amend all things reprovable. What we are, is by your favour. What we shall be, rests all in your applausive encouragements.

[Exeunt.

John Marston – A Short Biography

John Marston was born to John and Maria Marston née Guarsi, and baptised on October 7th, 1576 at Wardington, Oxfordshire. His father was an eminent lawyer of the Middle Temple who first practiced in London and then became the counsel to Coventry and later its steward.

Marston entered Brasenose College, Oxford in 1592 and earned his BA in 1594. By 1595, he was in London, living in the Middle Temple. His interests were in poetry and play writing, although his father's will of 1599 hopes that he would not further pursue such vanities.

His brief career in literature began with a foray into the then fashionable genres of erotic epyllion and satire; erotic plays for boy actors to be performed before educated young men and members of the inns of court.

In 1598, he published 'The Metamorphosis of Pigmalion's Image and Certaine Satyres', a book of poetry in imitation of, on the one hand, Ovid, and, on the other, the Satires of Juvenal. He also published 'The Scourge of Villanie', in 1598. (these were issued under the pseudonym "W. Kinsayder.") The satire in these books is even more savage and misanthropic than the prevailing norm for other satirists of the era. Marston's style sometimes bends to the point of unintelligibility: he believed that satire should be rough and obscure. Marston seems to have been enraged by Joseph Hall's claim to be the first satirist in English; Hall comes in for some indirect retribution later in one or more of his satires. Some see William Shakespeare's Thersites and Iago, as well as the mad speeches of King Lear as influenced by 'The Scourge of Villanie'.

Marston had, however, arrived on the literary scene as the fad for verse satire was coming under pressure from the authority's censors. Both the Archbishop of Canterbury and the Bishop of London banned 'The Scourge of Villanie' had it publicly burned, along with copies of works by other satirists, on 4th June 1599.

In September 1599, John Marston began to work for the famed Philip Henslowe as a playwright. Marston proved a good match for the private stage where boy players performed racy dramas for an audience of city gallants and young members of the Inns of Court.

'Histriomastix' has been regarded as his first play; performed by either the Children of Paul's or the students of the Middle Temple in around 1599. Its performance kicked off an episode in literary history commonly known as the 'War of the Theatres'; the literary feud between Marston, Jonson and Dekker that took place between 1599 and 1602.

Around 1600, Marston wrote 'Jack Drum's Entertainment' and 'Antonio and Mellida', and in 1601 he wrote 'Antonio's Revenge', a sequel to the latter play; all three were performed by the company at Paul's. In 1601, he contributed poems to Robert Chester's 'Love's Martyr'. For Henslowe, he may have also collaborated with Dekker, Day, and Haughton on 'Lust's Dominion'.

By 1601, he was well known in London literary circles, particularly in his role as enemy to the equally brilliant and difficult Ben Jonson. Jonson, who reported that Marston had accused him of sexual profligacy, satirized Marston as Clove in 'Every Man Out of His Humour', as Crispinus in 'Poetaster', and as Hedon in 'Cynthia's Revels'. Jonson thought Marston a false poet, a vain, careless writer who plagiarised the works of others and whose works were marked by bizarre diction and ugly neologisms. For his part, Marston used Jonson as the complacent, arrogant critic Brabant Senior in 'Jack Drum's Entertainment' and as the envious, misanthropic playwright and satirist Lampatho Doria in 'What You Will'.

'The Return from Parnassus (II)', an anonymous and satirical play performed at St. John's College, Cambridge in 1601 and 1602, characterised Marston as a poet whose writings see him 'pissing against the world'.

Jonson states that at one point their 'War' boiled over into the physical when he had beaten Marston and taken his pistol. However, the two playwrights were reconciled; Marston wrote a prefatory poem for Jonson's 'Sejanus' in 1605 and dedicated 'The Malcontent' to him.

Beyond this episode Marston's career continued to gather both strength, assets and followers. In 1603, he became a shareholder in the Children of Blackfriars company, at that time known for steadily pushing the boundaries of personal satire, violence, and lewdness on stage. He wrote and produced two plays with the company. The first was 'The Malcontent' in 1603, his most famous play. This work was originally written for the children at Blackfriars and was later taken over by the Kings' Men at the Globe, with additions by John Webster. His second play for the Blackfriars children was 'The Dutch Courtesan', a satire on lust and hypocrisy, in 1604-5.

In 1605, he worked with George Chapman and Ben Jonson on 'Eastward Ho', a satire of popular taste and the vain imaginings of wealth to be found in the colony of Virginia. Chapman and Jonson were arrested for, according to Jonson, a few clauses that offended the Scots, but Marston escaped any imprisonment. Their detainment was brief, and the charges were dropped.

He married Mary Wilkes in 1605, the daughter of the Reverend William Wilkes, one of the chaplains to King James.

In 1606, Marston seems to have had mixed fortunes with the king. At times offending and at others pleasing. In 'Parasitaster, or, The Fawn', he satirized the king specifically. However, in the summer of that year, he put on a production of 'The Dutch Courtesan' for the King of Denmark's visit, with a Latin verse on King James that was presented by hand to the king. Finally, in 1607, he wrote 'The Entertainment at Ashby', a masque for the Earl of Huntingdon.

Marston took the theatre world by surprise when he gave up writing plays in 1609 at the age of thirty-three. He sold his shares in the company of Blackfriars. His departure from the literary scene may have been because of further offence he gave to the king. The king suspended performances at Blackfriars and had Marston imprisoned.

After release he moved into his father-in-law's house to study philosophy. In 1609, he became a reader at the Bodleian library at Oxford. On 24th September he was made a deacon and then a priest on 24th December 1609. In October 1616, Marston was assigned the living of Christchurch, Hampshire.

He died (accounts vary) on either the 24th or 25th June 1634 in London and was buried in the Middle Temple Church.

Tombs at that time were often inscribed with 'Memoriae Sacrum' ('Sacred to the memory') and then the occupants name and a brief account of their achievements. According to Anthony à Wood Marston's tomb stone read 'Oblivioni Sacrum' ('Sacred to Oblivion'), which was probably composed by Marston, and both self-abasing and witty in upturning the tradition.

Marston's reputation through the centuries has varied widely, like that of most of the minor Renaissance dramatists. Both 'The Malcontent' and 'The Dutch Courtesan' remained on stage in altered forms throughout the Restoration.

After the Restoration, Marston's works were largely reduced to literary history. The general resemblance of 'The Malcontent' to 'Hamlet' and Marston's role in the 'War of the Theatres' ensured that his plays would receive some scholarly attention, but they were not performed, nor widely read.

The Romantic movement in English literature unevenly resuscitated Marston's reputation. In his lectures, William Hazlitt praised Marston's genius for satire; however, if the romantic critics were willing to grant Marston's best work a place among the great accomplishments of the age, they remained aware of his inconsistency, what Swinburne would later call his 'uneven and irregular demesne'.

In the twentieth century, however, a few critics were willing to consider Marston as a writer who was very much in control of the world he created. T. S. Eliot saw that this 'irregular demesne' was a part of Marston's world and that "It is ... by giving us the sense of something behind, more real than any of the personages and their action, that Marston establishes himself among the writers of genius".

Plays and production dates

Histriomastix (play), 1599
Antonio and Mellida, London, Paul's theater, 1599–1600.
Jack Drum's Entertainment, London, Paul's theater, 1599/1600.
Antonio's Revenge, London, Paul's theater, 1600.
What You Will, London, Paul's theater, 1601.
The Malcontent, London, Blackfriars Theatre, 1603–1604; Globe Theatre, 1604.
Parasitaster, or The Fawn, London, Blackfriars theater, 1604.
Eastward Ho, by Marston, George Chapman, and Ben Jonson, London, Blackfriars theater, 1604–1605.
The Dutch Courtesan, London, Blackfriars theater, 1605.
The Wonder of Women, or The Tragedy of Sophonisba, London, Blackfriars theater, 1606.
The Spectacle Presented to the Sacred Majesties of Great Britain, and Denmark as They Passed through London, London, 31 July 1606.
The Entertainment of the Dowager-Countess of Darby, Ashby-de-la-Zouch in Leicestershire, 1607.
The Insatiate Countess, by Marston and William Barksted, London, Whitefriars Theatre, c 1608.

Books

The Metamorphosis of Pigmalions Image. And Certaine Satyres.
The Scourge of Villanie. Three Bookes of Satyres (1598; revised and enlarged edition, 1599)
Jacke Drums Entertainment: Or, The Comedie of Pasquill and Katherine (1601)
Loves Martyr: or, Rosalins Complaint, by Marston, Ben Jonson, William Shakespeare, and George Chapman (1601)
The History of Antonio and Mellida (1602)
Antonios Revenge (1602)
The Malcontent (1604)
Eastward Hoe, by Marston, Chapman, and Jonson (1605)
The Dutch Courtezan (1605)
Parasitaster, or The Fawne (1606)
The Wonder of Women, or The Tragedie of Sophonisba (1606)
What You Will (1607)
Histrio-mastix: Or, The Player Whipt (1610)
The Insatiate Countesse, by Marston and William Barksted (1613)
The Workes of Mr. J. Marston (1633); republished as Tragedies and Comedies (1633)
Comedies, Tragi-comedies; & Tragedies, Nonce Collection (1652)
Lust's Dominion, or The Lascivious Queen (probably the same play as The Spanish Moor's Tragedy), by Marston, Thomas Dekker, John Day, and William Haughton (1657)

www.ingramcontent.com/pod-product-compliance
Lightning Source LLC
Chambersburg PA
CBHW021940040426
42448CB00008B/1166